U0809002

张海波
丁红朝　陶曙敎　吴思锋　王送军　刘伟臻
著

# 商务项目设计指南

Guidelines for the Design of Business Project

第2版
The 2nd Edition

暨南大學出版社
JINAN UNIVERSITY PRESS
中国·广州

**图书在版编目（CIP）数据**

商务项目设计指南 / 张海波等著. —2 版. —广州：暨南大学出版社，2016.1
ISBN 978-7-5668-1400-5

Ⅰ.①商… Ⅱ.①张… Ⅲ.①电子商务—项目管理—英语—写作
Ⅳ.① H315

中国版本图书馆 CIP 数据核字（2015）第 074224 号

出版发行：暨南大学出版社

地　址：中国广州暨南大学
电　话：总编室（8620）85221601
　　　　营销部（8620）85225284　85228291　85228292（邮购）
传　真：（8620）85221583（办公室）　85223774（营销部）
邮　编：510630
网　址：http: / /www. jnupress. com　http: / /press. jnu. edu. cn

排　版：广州市天河星辰文化发展部照排中心
印　刷：佛山市浩文彩色印刷有限公司

开　本：787mm × 960mm　1/16
印　张：9.625
字　数：194 千
版　次：2009 年 12 月第 1 版　2016 年 1 月第 2 版
印　次：2016 年 1 月第 3 次

定　价：25.00 元

（暨大版图书如有印装质量问题，请与出版社总编室联系调换）

# Contents

# Preface

There is no denying that aggressive marketing is crucial for any business to survive in today's dynamic business. The success of a business largely depends upon the ability to win contracts and establish strategic alliances that can boost the company's earning potential, income, and overall profitability. Given that the number of players in any field of business may be steadily increasing, it can be extremely challenging to attract new business. Those who want to realize their busi ness goals will need to carry out a rock-solid business project proposal.

In order to help students majoring in Business English carry out their own practical project in a business environment with a short business proposal in English used as their graduation thesis design, I spent more than two years researching on how to develop business projects and proposals, which, at length, resulted in this book—*Guidelines for the Design of a Business Project.*

As a guidance book, it mainly covers the process of developing business project proposals, including the definition and explanation of a particular technique or element that is used in preparing a business proposal, with some practical exercises and an example of how the technique is used in a sample proposal. It can also be helpful for those who are really running a business line or working with some other companies or organizations.

This book is obviously characterized by its step-by-step guiding process with easy-to-read explanations and corresponding samples available for both students and tutors to follow in each part. Further more, most of the samples are taken from the virtual business contexts, such as the Mini-Swallow Grocery Expansion Project, which in fact exists in any other university or college.

This book is made up of four chapters:

Chapter One involves the overview of a business project.

Chapter Two involves the essential components of a business project.

Chapter Three involves how to design your own project.

Chapter Four involves the sample for a business proposal.

Dear readers, just follow the guidelines together with the help of your tutors, you will be sure to accomplish your project assignment within the required time. After that, you will be capable of developing a real business project proposal for your future career by yourself.

张海波

2015 年 5 月于江门职业技术学院

# Acknowledgements

In the course of writing this book, I reviewed a variety of insightful opinions and comments from teachers and students, which are greatly helpful for me to make this book more readable and practical, and for which I am greatly appreciated. Special thanks go to my friends, classmates and business partners, reference book writers, at home and abroad, and those who used to give me formal and valuable comments, suggestions and materials for reference.

Victor Wang，general director of Val Technology，Inc. USA
Lisa Zeng，manager of Val Technology，Inc. USA
John Hilton，British expert
Xian Xibiao，assistant professor
Yang Qining & Cui Song
Hu Yiwu
江门职业技术学院
广州番禺职业技术学院
湖南交通职业技术学院
福建对外经济贸易职业技术学院

# Chapter One

# 第一章

## The Overview of a Business Project

## 商务项目概述

# Chapter One

## The Overview of a Business Project

You are going to leave the college after three or four years' study. As a Business English major, you have to get yourself prepared for your future business work. The writing of a business project proposal, which might be somewhat new to you, is one of the most important skills you should get good hold of. It's a good and practical way to test the ability of the students majoring in Business English. Anyhow, at the very beginning, you should learn what a business project is.

As a matter of fact, there are various ways to define a business project, for example:

(1) An **undertaking** that **encompasses** a set of tasks or activities having a **definable** starting point and well defined objectives. Usually each task has a planned **completion date** (due date) and **assigned** resources.

(2) A set of related tasks, which have a specific goal, often requires **concerted effort**. A project normally has strictly defined organization, **scheme**, **budget**, and time schedule. It is often financed by one **funding source**.

(3) A project is a series of planned activities carried out in order to achieve some **specific** objectives in a **specified** period of time.

(4) A project is a series of planned activities carried out in order to achieve a pre-specified change in a specified period of time.

**单词注释**

undertaking 任务，工作
encompass 包含，包括
definable 可规定的
completion date 完成日期
assigned 分配的
concerted effort 协同努力
scheme 方案
budget 预算
funding source 资金来源
specific 待定的
specified 设定的

What's more, you could find many more definitions about project from the Internet if you would like to. There is no denying that all sorts of activities can be treated as projects, as long as they meet the essential **qualifications** of a business project. Examples are :

- to set up an online store
- to hold an anniversary party
- to build a new house
- to plan an online advertisement
- to promote a new service
- to make a plan for a trip
- to change ways of producing line
- to expand new business for the company
- to design a business website
- to hold an important conference
- to **launch** a **promotion** of products
- to carry on a staff training program
- to write a novel
- to offer household management service
- to host a concert
- to establish a company
- to run a retail chain
- to develop a tourist destination

...

Just to name a few. All these above-mentioned activities can be perceived as projects, only a few of which are taken as general projects, while the majority are called business projects since they are all involved in business to some extent. So we can come to the conclusion that any activity that is involved in business is defined as a business project.

单词注释

qualification 资格，限定条件
launch 发起
promotion 促销，宣传

# Chapter Two

# 第二章

## The Essential Components of a Business Project

## 商务项目的构成要素

# Chapter Two

## The Essential Components of a Business Project

单词注释

component 要素；成分

context 环境；背景

You have to find out what essential **components** a project consists of before you can develop an effective business project. Generally speaking, all projects should share a series of common components listed below:

objectives
outputs
strategies and activities
a time-scale
resources
stakeholders
an environment

Next, we'll look into the above components one by one.

### 1. Objectives 目的

Here, of course, we just refer to the business project targets or purposes that people want to achieve when they want to carry out the project. Usually, we can divide objectives into two groups.

The first group are the wider aims or goals of the project: what people think or hope will happen in the general **context** if the project is successful.

The second group are the specific things or changes that people want the project to produce in order to help achieve the wider aims.

Suppose you are a grocery store owner who wants your business to be more **profitable** or to make more money. You might think it should be possible to double your profits, earning twice as much and it might be your wider goal or purpose. In order to make more money you might decide to expand the original shop or open a second one. This could be your specific objective—to expand the old store or to open a second store. So the project would be to expand the old shop or to open a second shop as you like.

We can also divide objectives into **quantitative objectives**, say, to increase ¥2,500 income a month, which you can measure directly in numbers, and **qualitative objectives**, for example, to improve the quality of the products for which different or indirect measurements may be quite necessary. However, you should never forget whichever kind of objective you have, you must know how you are going to measure it, otherwise you can hardly know whether you have achieved it or not.

This is the point in the course when you should be ready to propose a solution to the problems in the business context which your project is based on, and can discuss your objectives and agree on them with your tutor. This is a very important stage.

When planning a project and deciding on the objectives, it is important to remember that they need to be SMART, which stands for the following five words:

Specific, measurable, **agreed**, **realistic** and **timed-bound**.

Let's **put** them **across** one by one.

Specific: Be specific enough so that you know when you have achieved it. For example, an objective like "visit my parents more often" is not a specific one, because there is no point of **reference** as to what **counts as** "more often". A better one would be something like "visit my parents at least twice every month during this year". That would be more clear and **concrete**.

Let us say that the problem identified by **community** members is "lack of clean drinking water". The solution to this problem, the objective, then is "to bring clean drinking water to the community".

**单词注释**

profitable 有利可图的；可赢利的
quantitative objective 定量目标
qualitative objective 定性目标
agreed 一致的
realistic 现实的
time-bound 时限性
put...across 解释
reference 参照
count as 算作……
concrete 具体的
community 团队

You can **demonstrate** to the group the **vagueness** of this objective by going out of the room and returning with a single glass of water, showing it to them, "OK, here is some water. I have brought it to the community." Now, is the project complete? Have we achieved our goal?

Of course they might laugh or say that obviously they did not mean only a glass of water when they said "to bring clean drinking water to the community". Your reply is then that the project design or proposal must be very specific about each objective, so that there will be no room for different **interpretations**.

Therefore, objectives should be very precisely defined so that everyone knows exactly what has to be achieved.

Measurable: Your objectives must be measurable **in real terms**. Otherwise you might make people confused at what you say. For instance, if you say your objective is to make more money, it would be hardly measurable because the word "more" is an **ambiguity**. It would be very difficult to estimate the exact amount of money. How do you know when you reach "more"? However, if you say your objective is to earn 100% more money, then it is measurable. You know when you have reached the target. In the case of a software project, it is not enough to say that you will design a better and faster software. You need to explain in real terms how fast it will work or what precise **features** will make it better.

Agreed: Objectives must be acceptable to everyone concerned with the project. If your partner in the business doesn't agree with you on the objectives, the project will either never start or **be doomed to** fail from the beginning. The objectives for the software project need to be agreed, not just by you and your design team, but by the customers as well.

Realistic: It would be rather silly to set yourself an objective that you can't achieve from the beginning. Let us imagine that you agree to develop the **software package** so that it can be used in

**单词注释**

demonstrate 说明，解释
vagueness 模糊不清
interpretation 解释
measurable 可测性
in real terms 按实际
ambiguity 含混不清的说法
feature 特色，特性
be doomed to 注定会……
software package 软件包

France, but there is no one in your team who knows French or anything about French **accounting systems**. In this case the project objectives are undoubtedly not realistic and the project will certainly be a failure.

Time-bound: It is important that you decide by when you expect the project to be completed. Most contracts require you to deliver by a certain date and there may be **penalties** if you are late. If you don't plan the time requirements thoroughly and accurately, you will probably find that you will run out of money before you accomplish your goal. For example, if you have borrowed money from the bank to pay your staff until the new software package is delivered and paid for, you will have to pay interest on the money until you can pay it back. And of course you can't start to pay the money back to the bank until you have been paid by the company which ordered the software. If the development of the software is delayed, you will have to find still more money to keep the bank happy and perhaps run into serious debt, or even get **bankrupt**.

## 2. Outputs 产出

The outputs of a project are the things which only exist after the project is completed. Often they are **physical** things produced by a project, such as a new computer, but they can also be things which are less concrete, like staff who have new qualifications. In previous example of the shopkeeper, the main output of the project would be a second shop, which does not exist before the project but now does. In a different project, if your objective is to improve the happiness of your staff by designing smart new **uniforms** for them, one output would be the new uniforms. If you decide to measure the happiness of your staff by counting the number of times they are absent from work, an output might be a **reduction** in the number of days when your staff are sick or don't come to work. If you are in charge of the Students' Union, your objective is to get a collection of

**单词注释**

accounting system 会计制度
penalty 处罚，刑罚
bankrupt 破产的
physical 物质的；有形的
uniform 制服
reduction 减少

yearly reports and suggestions or plans for the year to come, then the output should be the yearly conference. If you are out of job, and want to be your own boss, one output is to establish your initial business company. If the original production line is too slow to meet the demand of the market , you should replace the production line with a new one which would be the output.

## 3. Strategies and Activities 策略与实施

A Strategy is a long-term plan of action designed to achieve a particular goal, most often "to win". Strategy is **differentiated** from **tactics** or immediate actions with resources at hand by its nature of being **extensively premeditated**, and often practically **rehearsed**. Strategies are used to make the problem easier to understand and solve. In brief, a strategy is the means you take to produce the outputs.

Activities refer to concrete actions taken or work performed through which inputs, such as funds, technical **assistance** and other types of resources are **mobilized** to produce specific outputs. It is about what exact things should be done in order to achieve the goal.

We can see various kinds of activities in different projects, for example, asking for a loan, ordering new equipment, **negotiating** with the related persons, carrying out some marketing investigation or research, making focus group reports, seeking experts' suggestions or opinions, looking for some reliable business partners, conducting current business state analysis, having a picture of customer profiles, getting the **cost breakdown** done, evaluating the risks, and so on. No matter what an activity might be, it is so indispensable in your project that can never be ignored.

**单词注释**

differentiate 区别
tactic 策略；战术
extensively 全面地
premeditate 事先策划
rehearse 演练
assistance 支持；帮助
mobilize 调动
negotiate 协商
cost breakdown 成本核算

## 4. A Time-scale 时刻表

All projects have time-scales, in other words, there is a definite end-date or time by which the project is to achieve its objectives. In this respect, projects **are** often **contrasted with** programs, which have no definite end-date.

In setting the time-scale of a project, a range of different factors have to be taken into consideration. These include:

A. The **nature** of the objectives. Some can be achieved quickly, others require more time. That is because some projects are small and simple, so they need only a small amount of time to complete, while some are big and complicated, and might cause a long time to finish.

B. The financial and human resources available.

C. The **logistics** of a project. Certain aspects of a project may require defined amounts of time which cannot be changed.

D. The environment in which the project is to be carried out. The environment has physical, social and political **dimensions**, such as the weather, geography, transportations, the communications, the local economic status, local trading policies, the political situation, etc. You have to think about each of these aspects of the environment.

E. The "people" factor. People are not machines and the **unpredictability** that arises from this also has to be taken into consideration. For instance, some workers happen to be suffering from some sickness, some hand in their **resignations** because of the unsatisfactory pay or working conditions, some are not so professional, some are not so honest and might hurt your business images, some are lazy which may cause delay while carrying out your project.

## 5. Resources 资源

In order to carry out a project, resources of various kinds are needed, but if they are not available, then either the project cannot be undertaken at all or the necessary resources need to be found from somewhere.

The resources include:

A. Financial resources. Is sufficient money available at the

单词注释

be contrasted with...
与……形成对比
nature 本质
logistics 组织工作
dimension 因素
unpredictability
不可预测性
resignation 辞呈

times when it is needed? This is a critical problem to be solved at first.

B. Human resources. Are the necessary people available and willing to work for you, and do they have enough time to **devote to** the project?

C. Material resources. These may include such things as buildings, equipment, software, transport, **telecommunications**, etc.

## 6. Stakeholders 利益相关者

A stakeholder is any person or organization who can be **positively** or **negatively impacted** by, or cause an impact on the actions of a company.

These are all the people, **institutions** or organizations which have interests in the project being carried out (or in certain cases not being carried out). They can be broadly divided into four groups: clients, customers, project staff and others.

Clients include the people who provide funds for the project. They may be yourself, your family, a bank, or your shareholders and the people or organizations that want you to carry out the project.

Customers include the target **recipients** of the project. They may be customers, teachers, students, local residents, children, blue-collar workers, middle class, **pregnant** women, or any other group for whom the project is being carried out.

Project staff include the project management team. They may be **internal** or **external** to the project. Which means that the managers of the project may also be members of the project team (internal), or may not be directly involved in carrying out the project themselves (external). The project implementation team are also included—those who will actually carry out the work.

Other stakeholders, also called indirect stakeholders, include the **host body**, for example:

A. The owner of the building in which your business is located

**单词注释**

devote to 投入；致力于
telecommunications 通信设备
positively 正面地
negatively 负面地
impact 影响
institution 机构
recipient 接受者
pregnant 怀孕的
internal 内部的
external 外部的
host body 主体

and to whom you pay rent.

B. People or organizations whose permission or agreement may be needed for the project to be carried out. They might include government departments or the police; the formers will offer you the right or license to do business, while the latter will protect your business and your life.

C. Other individuals, for example, local residents. If you have a bar, they might not be very happy if loud music was played every night in the bar, and start complaining to the police and bring troubles to your project.

## 7. An Environment 环境

Projects rarely take place in **isolation** or in a **vacuum**. They take place in an environment and may be affected by it. Features of the environment that may need to be taken into consideration are:

A. Physical—Is there a suitable road near your factory so that raw materials can be delivered and products can be sent to your customers without difficulties?

B. Economic—Is the economic situation favorable for the project? Do people want to **invest**, or are they keeping their money in the bank? What is the present GDP? How much do the people there spend in a year? etc.

C. Social—Will your product **appeal to** the customers, or will it be **rejected** because it is not socially acceptable? etc.

D. Political—Do government policies support the development of your kind of business? Are there any other **pressures** coming from **authority** for you to do or not to do certain things? etc.

**单词注释**

isolation 隔离（区）
vacuum 真空
invest 投资
appeal to 对……有吸引力的
reject 拒绝
pressure 压力
authority 当权

# Chapter Three

# 第三章

## How to Design Your Own Project

## 如何设计商务项目

# Chapter Three

## How to Design Your Own Project

In this section, you will learn what you have to do for your own project. The following guidelines will help you understand a number of different things that are commonly done in getting a proposal prepared for a business project. You will not be asked to do all of them, but you'd better do enough of them to be able to write a simple business project proposal.

Since you are a graduating student, your project will be expected to run a small business. You should first be familiar with such a small one so that you can easily produce a simple business proposal for it. And you should keep in mind that your project could be carried out only by careful and clear planning so as to make your business bigger, better, more profitable and more efficient. Don't worry, you are not being asked to prepare a real proposal, of course, but it should be as realistic as possible. Here are the 8 stages of a project design for you to refer to.

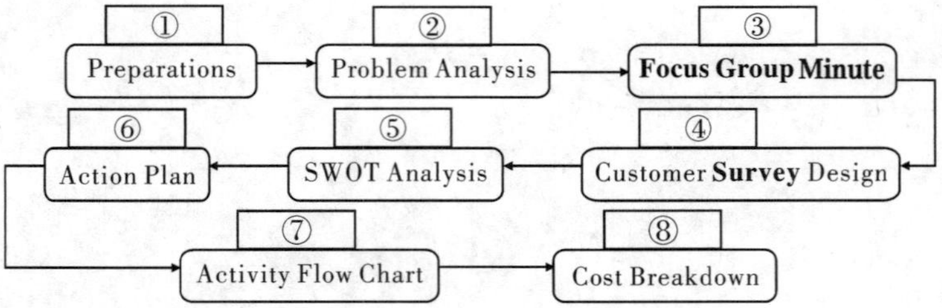


**单词注释**

focus group 核心小组
minute 纪要
survey 调查

## Stage 1 Preparations 准备工作

This part involves two subjects: one is to choose a right project; the other is to present problems. You are required to talk about the two subjects with your **tutor.**

### (1) Choose a right project.（选题）

It is your **initial task** to decide on the business that you want to use as the basis for your business project proposal. In agreement with your tutor, you can choose any business you like, but you are strongly suggested to choose a business you know well about, or can have easy access to, so that you can get the information you need in a fairly easy and practical way.

Nevertheless, if you are working in a certain business for the time being, you could, of course, take advantage of it as a favorable condition for your project. Yet, if you think where you work is not suitable, you'd better just pick a small commercial business near where you live or you often go to.

Don't worry if you cannot get the exact information you want about the business. For example, if a shopkeeper is not willing to let you stay in the company and visit the working place or the accountant refuses to show you their financial data, you can **estimate** or invent the information by your imagination. This will be perfectly acceptable as long as the information you give is realistic and not too outrageous. For instance, you might say your small shop takes up an area of 35 square meters (but not 3, 500, which is too large to be true), the yearly income reaches RMB500,000 (but not RMB 5,000,000, which is impossible for a small business to reach), you may say there are 20 employees in your company (but not 2,000).

### (2) Present problems.（亟须解决的问题）

Now it's time for you to find out how a project in a business situation can be planned since we have had a look at the essential elements of a project.

The first thing that needs to be done is to identify the prob-

**单词注释**

tutor 指导老师
initial task 初始任务
estimate 估量

lems, which the project will solve or help solve.

Suppose that the basic target of any business is to make more money in the future than it does at present, then how to achieve this target is sure to be the very problem.

The second thing we have to do is to be sure that we know clearly and exactly what is happening in the business. We have to know where we start, otherwise we won't know whether we have achieved anything at the end of our project. Just as a map is not of much use if you don't know where you are—to get to a place you have to start somewhere—so a project won't be so much useful unless you know where the start point is.

## Stage 2 Problem Analysis 分析问题

This is the most complicated and heavy section of all the eight stages, because a great deal of written work is contained in it. Since you **identify** various problems **occurring** in your current business and find how these problems occur, it is quite necessary for you to carry out a lot of research tasks so as to achieve the objectives for your project, which is called "problem analysis" or "business analysis". Normally there are three aspects we have to investigate in order to be clear about the current state of your business as follows:

### (1) The current state of the business.（公司现状）

This includes looking into and checking the **cash flow** of the business, that is how much money comes weekly or monthly and how much goes out. It also means looking at the situation concerning **creditors** and **debtors**—how much money the business owes to **suppliers** or to the bank, and how much money is owed to the business. All these information should be available to the businessman from the financial records of the business. Usually you can find these data from the company's monthly or yearly financial report.

### (2) Current business analysis.（当前业务分析）

What kind of products sell fast and regularly and what sell slowly but regularly? Are there things in the store, which you sell

**单词注释**

identify 识别，认清
occur 出现
cash flow 现金周转
creditor 债权人，贷方
debtor 债务人，借方
supplier 供应商

only occasionally? If a shopkeeper keeps records like this, they will help decide how often to order more stock and how much to order each time. They will also help in decisions to stop selling things that sit on the shelf for a long time and things which you have paid for but can not get your money back by selling them.

(3) Customer profiles.（顾客状况）

What kind of people are your customers? Are they local residents or people who are only passing through your area? Are they professional people or ordinary working people? Students or housewives? Children or adults? Mostly men or mostly women? Knowing what kind of people coming to your store helps you decide what you should sell, and a sensible shopkeeper will collect this kind of information as much as possible.

You might now have a clear idea of the present **status** of the business. And you are required to complete the first task according to the sample given below.

单词注释

status 状况
major in 主营
foodstuff 食品
household supply 家庭用品

***Note:** For all the samples for assignments, we have taken the example of a small store on a college campus , which is called Mini-Swallow Grocery. You are free to choose any similar small business such as a book store , a flower shop, a beauty parlor, a fashion shop, a small café bar or a small delicious restaurant, an online company, and so on. The most important thing is that you know it quite well so that you can easily get access to the basic information you might need to develop your proposal.

※A Sample for Assignment 1

**The Min-Swallow Grocery Expansion Project**

1. The current state of the business

Mini-Swallow Grocery, established in 2005, is a privately owned business which lies on the campus of Jiangmen Polytechnic. It **majors** mainly **in foodstuffs**, various **household supplies** and office supplies for students, teachers, staff and local residents. It is located between the police station and

Student Dormitory 2 and right in the center of the campus by the West River. A large number of customers would pay a visit to it every day.

However, the store only **takes up** an area of 80 square meters, in which only two thirds can be used as the working area and one third the storage room, which is greatly preventing the store from expanding its services. The manager tried many times to offer a wider range of services, but failed each time because of the narrow space, which caused 20% of the revenue down in 2013, and thus makes us urgently feel it is high time to expand the store before it is too late.

2. Current business analysis

The major business of the store now is selling foodstuffs, various household supplies and office supplies for students, teachers and staff and local residents. In normal case, the store's warehouse can keep a stock of 50, 000 pieces of goods, which is now getting much farther from enough due to the growing number of students and teachers and staff year by year.

The financial **performance** has improved a good deal since the store opened. The **revenue** in 2008, at 500, 000 yuan, increased by 43% over the 2007 level of 350, 000 yuan.

Profits went up by 25%, while costs went down by 8%, thanks to the effective cost-cutting measures initiated at the beginning of 2008. The **inventory turnover ratio** has reached 7 times and the **profit margin** on sales 5%, well above the average of five times and 4% **respectively**.

As you know, the store was **granted** the first loan of RMB 350,000 for **launching business** in 2005. By the end of 2007, half of the loan had been paid back, nearly one year ahead of the schedule due to the increased **enrollment** during the past two years. The store paid off the debt by the end of 2009 based on the current cash flow.

There are only 10 workers in the store, including one manager, one accountant, 7 shop assistants and one door keeper. They are always very busy.

This fact shows we are badly in need of hands.

3. Customer profiles

The majority of the customers of the store are students, including the following kinds:

◇**Undergraduates**, who **account for** 80% of the student population.

◇**Full-time graduate students**, who occupy a small percentage of the enrollment. However, the number of graduate students is growing much

**单词注释**

take up 占据
performance 业绩
revenue 收入；收益
inventory turnover ratio 库存周转率
profit margin 利润率
respectively 分别地
grant 授予；同意；承认
launch business 开办商店
enrollment 招生
undergraduate 大学生
account for 占据
full-time graduate student 全日制本科毕业生

faster than that of undergraduates, because more and more **job vacancies** are only open to **candidates** with a master's degree.

◇Part-time graduate students, who only come to school at weekends.

◇**Trainees**, who come to school to attend intensive training programs on a specific subject.

◇Foreign students, who are either studying for a college degree or to improve their Chinese.

Non-student customers include:

◇Teachers, staff, and retirees of the college.

◇Residents living around the college.

◇Workers from the factories around.

◇Part-time employees in the college such as the peasants who work as cleaners and gardeners.

4. Complaints and requests from customers

It is the lack of space that makes the store unable to increase its stock, or hire more employees to expand its services. That's why customers often express their dissatisfaction. Their main complaints are as follows:

◇The store is too small. They often have to stay in line, waiting for service. Let alone enjoy wandering around **leisurely**.

◇It is too far away from the students' dormitories. It is noisy and **smelly** during meal times because the students' dining hall stands too close to it.

◇The store is **stuffy**. They can hardly stay long in the store.

◇Sometimes they have to go out of campus to get things that could not be provided in the store, such as phone cards, books, magazines, computer hardware and software, etc.

◇The number of the shop assistants is far from enough. Besides, they are not so professional and kind as they are expected.

◇Customers often inquire if the store could offer college-branded items such as T-shirts, calendars, postcards, envelops, letter-sheets, etc.

◇A **photocopying** service is wanted by many customers since there is no such a kind of service around, which often makes them go out of the campus.

**单词注释**

job vacancy 职务空缺
candidate 候选人
trainee 受训人员
leisurely 从容地，悠闲地
smelly 有异味的
stuffy 不通气的
photocopying 复印

## Your Assignment 1

You should by now have agreed with your tutor on the small business which you are going to use as the basis of your own project. You need to carry out the first task.

Here are some additional hints for you to go by in the course of your doing the first assignment.

First of all, you should carry out as far as you can an analysis of the business. Unless you are very fortunate, you may not be able to get the real and accurate figures for the financial state of the business. Don't worry. This doesn't matter too much. What you should do is to make realistic estimates of the finances of the business, which could be used as your support information later.

Then how can you achieve this? Here are the hints:

① By going into any shop and asking how much the goods cost, you can easily find out what prices the shop sells things for.

② Make a **sensible** estimate of the amount the shop sells in a week and multiply this by 50 to get a figure for the year. Then you can calculate the annual **income** of the shop.

③ Assume that the difference between what the shop pays for its goods and the price it sells them for—the mark-up—is 100%, and calculate how much the shop spends on buying its stock for the year, which is **stock cost**.

④ Make sensible estimates of the cost of things like wages for staff, rent and so on, which add up to **running cost**. They don't have to be real figures, just ones that are realistic and possible.

⑤ You can now **subtract** the figures for buying stock and for other costs from the figure for the annual income and you will have a realistic figure for the profit the shop makes. Here is the counting **formula**:

Profit = Income − (Stock Cost + Running Cost)

***Note**: These are the basic figures you can use in carrying out the rest of your project. Actually we don't demand that these figures have to be accurate.Instead, they just look possible. That would be quite enough.

**单词注释**

sensible 切合实际的
income 收入
stock cost 库存成本
running cost运营成本
subtract 减去，扣掉
formula 公式

Now that you know what the current business state is, you need to start looking at the future a little bit. Here you will learn what the customers of the store think about it, and what they would like to see being sold in the store which the store does not sell at present.

In this section, an analysis of unsatisfied customer requests is necessary to be listed as the sample shows above.

## Stage 3 Focus Group Minute 核心小组座谈纪要

A focus group is a small number of your customers (usually about 8–10), who are willing to meet together and tell you what they think about your business. The number of people need not be very large, but people in the group should be a **representative** and uniform sample of your customers. Each group should represent a clearly defined group of your customers. In other words, if half of your customers are housewives and half are students, then you might decide to have two separate focus groups. One would be made up of housewives and the other of students. Or you might think that the needs of female students are different from the needs of male students. In this case you might set up three focus groups—one of housewives, one of male students and one of female students. Depending on the kind of business you run and the range of your customers, you might want to have focus groups of other categories, such as age, nationality, job-type, sex, class, region, profession, hobby, interest, yearly income, community, etc.

Before you have a meeting with a focus group, you should study a number of questions about your business so as to find the answers to them, and you should also ask for their suggestions about the development of the business. Don't forget you need their **criticisms** as well as their positive suggestions. The discussion should be as free as possible so that you can get the maximum information from each group.

单词注释

representative 有代表性的
criticism 批评
maximum 最多的

## ※A Sample for Assignment 2

### Focus Group Minute

In order to get a clear picture of the views and opinions of customers, five focus groups were organized. The focus groups were as follows:

Group 1: 10 undergraduate students;

Group 2: 8 graduate students;

Group 3: 8 university staff;

Group 4: 7 workers nearby;

Group 5: 7 local residents.

Since each of these categories of customer might have different expectations, views and needs, **separate** focus groups would be **desirable**. However, we found that separate focus groups of men and women were not used, for there would be no **significant** differences of opinion between them in a college environment.

Although basic list of questions was prepared beforehand, the discussions with each focus group were allowed to be free and open.

Questions prepared are:

◇How many times do you visit the grocery store in a week?

◇How do you feel each time you pay a visit to the grocery store?

◇Do you usually find the goods you need?

◇What do you do when you can't find what you are looking for in the store?

◇What kinds of items that are not offered now that you or your friends would like to buy?

◇What do you think of the prices the grocery store offers?

◇What kind of additional services would you like to see if the store could expand its services in the future?

◇What most often disappoints you when you come to the store?

◇What do you think of the business hours at present?

◇Do you think the shop assistants are helpful?

◇How do you expect the store to be **remodeled** when it reopens?

The responses to the questions above were positive and **constructive** for this expansion project.

Complaints gathered from the focus groups are:

**单词注释**

separate 分别的
desirable 可取的
significant 重大的
remodel 改造
constructive 具有建设性的

◇The space of the store is so small that it is a suffering rather than an enjoyment to visit it.

◇The shop assistants, lacking experience of working in a grocery store, often failed to give appropriate help when asked to do so.

◇Sometimes they have to go out of campus to get things that could not be provided in the store, such as phone cards, books, magazines, computer hardware and software, etc.

◇The present business hours are rather short. Students would prefer to visit the store after evening study sessions.

◇The number of the shop-assistants is far from enough. Besides, they are not so professional and kind as they are expected to be.

Suggestions gathered from the focus groups are:

◇The space of the store should be expanded at least half of the present size.

◇A photocopier and a printer as well as a public telephone should be **installed**.

◇The **aisles** between the goods-shelves should be wider so as to let customers have enough walking space.

◇It's necessary to get the present store remodeled, which should be simple but comfortable.

◇Lighting and **ventilation** in the expanded store should be firstclass.

◇The management should watch closely the latest book reviews in order to have the latest and best books in stock.

◇The store should try to offer college-branded items such as T-shirts, calendars, postcards, envelops, letter-sheets, etc.

单词注释

install 安装
aisle（席位间的）通道
ventilation 通风

## Your Assignment 2

Do your assignment 2—"Focus Group Minute".

In the second assignment, you have got two parts to complete:

### 1. Results 结果

Write a report about what you think the results of a focus group discussion about the business you have chosen might be. Obviously, you will not be able to carry out a real focus group study, but you can use your own opinions about the business, and those of any people you know who visit the shop. You could even talk to the owner of the business or someone who works there and get his or her ideas. You can also use your imagination to think about other possible opinions. The important thing, once again, is to make the criticisms and suggestions as realistic as possible.

Write this report carefully, as you will have to give it to your tutor at the end of this period.

### 2. Complaints and Suggestions 意见和建议

From everything you have done so far, make a list of all the complaints and suggestions about the business, whether they are real or imaginary. This list will help you decide on the objectives for your proposed business project.

## Stage 4 Customer Survey Design 设计顾客问卷调查

The first **principle** of quality management is listening to your customers. Customer surveying is an essential listening tool that can **yield** information about customer expectations, customer satisfaction and strategies for improvement.

Designing **sound** survey is a basic skill you should learn. By completing 12 basic steps of survey design, you are able to gather useful, timely and accurate customer information from your surveys.

Quality surveys are built on two types of **expertise**: your business process knowledge plus a survey specialist's technical knowledge. As a business process participant, you are responsible for several of the steps that **profoundly** affect the scope, type and quality of any survey effort .

Here step-by-step guidelines are provided to assist you and your organization in developing and implementing an effective survey. You need to make 12 key decisions in three areas: establishing goals and objectives, constructing the survey instrument and **finalizing** survey logistics.

### (1) Establishing goals and objectives.(树立目标)

The most important and often the most challenging part of survey

**单词注释**

principle 原则
yield 提供
sound 完整的；健全的
expertise 专门技术
profoundly 深远地
finalize 定案

design is **clarifying** survey **intent** and **scope**. This is the essential part of your business knowledge because survey specialists can't read your mind and only you know what is the most important thing to your business or program.

Step 1: Determine survey purpose. The most critical part of survey design is a clearly defined **statement** of purpose and a well-structured view of what you will do with your newly acquired information. Surveys are decision-making tools. They have little value if you are not clear on the decisions your survey will support. Completing the following sentences to **formalize** your intent.

◇Why I want to do a survey is because ________________.

◇I intend to use the information I am seeking by __________.

◇The information to be gathered will enable me to decide ____ ______________________________________________.

◇I am prepared to implement change as a result of this survey because __________________________________________.

Your responses provide a **compass**, like the **mission** statement for your work unit, that will keep the project focused. A clear purpose guides the remaining survey design elements and emphasizes action based on results. One of the worst outcomes is collecting information that is never acted upon.

Step 2: Identify who will use the results and how they communicate. Surveys are communication tools. It is important to understand who will use the survey results and what type of information they respond to. Pay attention to the common **pitfall** of assuming others share your judgement of data. Although marketing staff may be comfortable with focus group results, a technical **audience** may want **statistics**. Leaders often want both numbers and human-interest **perspectives** when making decisions. Thus, a quantitative survey **paired with** selected case studies can be the most **compelling** for this group.

Complete the following statements which will help you define the survey audience.

**单词注释**

clarify 阐明
intent 意图
scope 范围
statement 陈述
formalize 使定型
compass 指南针
mission 使命
pitfall 陷阱
audience 受众
statistics 统计数据
perspective 看法
pair with 与……结合
compelling 令人信服的

◇The users of the survey results include________________.

◇The group (s) I will provide with information include______ ______________________________________________________.

◇They want the information in order to__________________.

◇The way (s) they like to receive information include______ ______________________________________________________.

**Step 3:** Identify what specific information is needed and when this next level of **refinement** identifies and double-checks the information needed from the survey process. Completing the following statements helps you **prioritize** your information needs.

◇The information I really need is______________________.

◇I need this information because______________________.

◇My **top-priority** information needs are__________________.

Identify all the information above that will enable you to make decisions and take action.

Be specific. Identify every element of data that will be collected with its added value. Avoid the **tendency** to gather information that is merely interesting or might be good to know.

Develop specific research questions that need to be answered. For example, if you are looking for information on a proposed product, identify the new product's elements and the concerns you have about each of them. Also, consider how your choice of survey information will protect the **participants' privacy**.

Once you have prioritized your information needs, determine when surveying should begin and how often it should occur. Answering the following questions will help you decide.

◇How soon will I need information from this survey?

◇How often does significant change occur in my process, my customers or their lives or in the environment in which this process operates?

◇How often do I need updated information to manage my process or program?

◇How often do survey users need updated information?

**单词注释**

refinement 细化
prioritize 把……区分优先次序
top-priority 最优先的
tendency 倾向
participant 参与者
privacy 隐私

The survey start date may be driven by important decisions you need to make, or by how much time you are willing to devote to planning a long-term survey effort.

Determine how often to survey by weighing the potential benefit **derived from** resurveying versus the investment in resources—both yours and your customers'. As a rule, the time period between surveys should be short enough to give you reliable information, yet long enough that your customers will not feel bothered. Several factors drive survey **frequency**, including survey length and **complexity**, changes in your customer base, changes in your service or product delivery process, and **seasonality** of services or products.

Step 4: Determine resource requirements. Ideally, resources devoted to your survey will be driven by the importance of the decisions you will make based on the data. Consider the following questions when scoping your resource requirements:

◇What is the value of the information I am seeking?

◇What are the potential consequences of the decisions I will make based on this information?

◇What is the cost of not having survey data?

◇What staff and other resources are currently available?

◇What staff and other resources do I need?

Then determine the resource requirements by identifying the staff and financial resources that can be devoted to the project. It is important to agree about resource issues to ensure you have the capability to deliver a survey that meets your overall expectations. You may have internal resources, such as trained interviewers or data analysts. If not, consider whether you are willing to **contract out** for these services. Limitations on resource requirements will shape the entire survey design process.

Step 5: Determine who should conduct the survey. Even if you have the in-house capability to conduct a survey, sometimes it is important to use a **neutral** third party. The main benefits are **credibility** and **candor**. In some cases, survey users or respondents

单词注释

derive from 由来
frequency 频率
complexity 复杂度
seasonality 季候性
contract out 外包
neutral 中立的，中性的
credibility 可信度
candor 真诚，直率

may believe that your organization lacks objectivity in collecting or reporting survey results. Survey users may find a study conducted by an independent third party more credible than the one you conduct yourself. In other cases, survey respondents may withhold information if they are speaking to a seemingly "interested party" about **sensitive issues.**

Even if you select an outside **consultant**, be sure to complete the survey design steps that follow. Your answers to the remaining questions will help the firm you select complete the work with excellence.

(2) Constructing the survey instrument.（构建调查手段）

Now you have entered the stages where it is important to tap into internal or external survey expertise. Depending on the size and complexity of your survey, you may need to involve a survey expert throughout the remaining steps of the survey planning process.

Step 6: Determine who has the information you need . Once you have identified information and presentation needs, you should consider whom to survey. This is called selecting the "sample **frame**" . In most cases, you will gather data from one or more **subsets** of the entire universe of people you can contact. By making an **intelligent** choice of whom to survey, your results will be accurate and your survey costs will be lower. Consider the following questions:

◇Who has the information I need?

◇Is my customer base made up of two or more **discrete** groups, or are all my customers fairly similar?

◇Who decides whether to use my products or services?

◇Do I have their current addresses or phone numbers?

◇What is (are) included in the key group(s) I need information from?

◇Shall I **randomly** sample from my entire customer base or survey only certain types of customers?

It is important to understand who your sample represents in order to draw appropriate conclusions from the data. If you wish to **generalize**

**单词注释**

sensitive issue 敏感问题
consultant 顾问
instrument 手段，工具
frame 框架
subset 子集
intelligent 明智的
discrete 独立的
randomly 随机地
generalize 推断；概括

from the sample to the population it represents, the sample must be randomly selected. Random selection tends to **assure** the most representative sample ( and will probably **generate** the highest credibility among users) , but is not necessary or desirable in every case. Depending on your overall customer base or the decisions you are facing, you may want to **concentrate** your survey on a particular segment rather than a random selection of your entire customer base. This is especially true if your customer base is characterized by distinct segments rather than homogeneity.

Step 7: Select an appropriate survey type. There are several types of survey formats you could use to obtain the information:

Face-to-face interviews are often conducted to explore issues that are not easily understood and when information cannot be gathered from a written or telephone survey. Face-to-face interviews also allow the interviewer to assess nonverbal responses and ask follow-up questions. These interviews are often used to gain **insight** into customer needs and requirements as well as to determine which services are most important to them.

Telephone surveys consist of a series of questions and answers presented in strict **sequence** by a trained interviewer. Some survey organizations use computer-aided telephone **interviewing** software. The strength of telephone surveys lies in their interactive nature. Respondents can ask for clarification about the questions, and surveyors can quickly spot any problems with survey **administration**.

Written surveys are the most commonly used survey type because of their lower cost and labor requirements. A written survey allows the customer to have more time to respond, but there is no opportunity to clarify their intent. Because no interviewer is available to coach the respondent through the questions, it is very important for questions to be ordered properly and for clear directions to be given.

Focus groups are small-group conversations **moderated** by a neutral **facilitator**. They can provide valuable, in-depth and detailed reactions to new **concepts** and ideas. Questions tend to be open-

**单词注释**

assure 确保
generate 产生
concentrate 集中
insight 洞察；深刻见解
sequence 顺序
interview 访谈
administration 部门
moderate 主持；节制
facilitator 主持者
concept 概念

ended. The results are largely qualitative and cannot be generalized to the entire population unless extreme care is taken when **recruiting respondents**. One use of focus groups is to provide a quick and fairly inexpensive way to identify the issues to be **addressed** in a **subsequent** mail-out or telephone survey.

Key informant interviews are face-to-face or telephone interviews with leaders in a field whose responses can be assumed to apply generally to others in that field. Open-ended or quantitative questions can be used.

The survey method you select depends largely on the time available, customer characteristics, the information you wish to obtain and the costs you are willing to incur. Consider the following questions when choosing a survey type:

◇What format will get the needed information at the lowest cost and effort, and within the time frame I need?

◇How will limitations of survey types impact my ability to make key decisions?

Mail surveys can suffer from low response rates. Ways to **boost** survey returns include:

Reducing respondent **barriers** to survey return through such means as short surveys (faster to fill out) and postage-paid, **pre-addressed** mailers (easier to mail).

Using postcard or telephone reminders to follow up with respondents who have not returned their surveys.

Providing **incentives**, such as gifts or chances to win prizes, for returning surveys.

In most cases, surveys personally and courteously handed to customers during the service-delivery process have higher response rates. Surveys available for pick-up at the service-delivery location are often only completed by customers who have had a very favorable or a very unfavorable experience. This, of course, creates a different type of **bias**.

Telephone surveys provide the fastest **turnaround** and allow

**单词注释**

recruit 征求
respondent 调查对象
address 讨论
subsequent 随后的
boost 推进，提高
barrier 障碍
pre-addressed 预先指明的
incentive 鼓励措施
bias 偏爱，爱好，癖好
turnaround 好转

you to **troubleshoot** problems not **detected** in the **pretest**. Telephone surveys are best used when all **segments** of the survey population are known to have telephones and should be conducted during the time of day when respondents will be available to talk, which may be after 5: 00 p.m.

Step 8: Design the survey questions. Survey results will be meaningless unless you ask the right questions. Ideally, they are based on the steps outlined above and on the survey and analysis **approaches** employed. Consider the following when designing questions:

◇How is this question **relevant to** the purpose of the survey?

◇Is the question clearly worded?

◇Will the question be easily understood by the customers?

The question must contain enough specifics so that the **respondents** can give a meaningful answer. Compare, for example, the following examples: How would you rate our service? How would you rate the timeliness of our computer-repair services? Answers to the former will be difficult to act upon, while answers to the latter tell you clearly what, if anything, needs to change.

Types of questions: Two types of questions are generally asked on written surveys—open questions and closed questions. Open questions allow the customer to respond to the question in his or her own words. They can be a rich source of information, especially when you may not know all the possible answers that respondents might choose. However, you must consider how you will analyze the results of open questions, for you will need a **coding system** to **quantify** open-question responses.

Closed questions offer the customer a choice of specific responses from which to select. Multiple choice, rating scale and yes/no questions are examples of closed questions.

The questions you ask your customers must be properly worded in order to achieve good end results. Try to begin all of your questions with how, what, when, where, why or do. Avoid the following:

**单词注释**

troubleshoot 排除困难
detect 检测到；发现
pretest 预先试验（测试）
segment 部分
approach 方法，方式
relevant to 与……相关
respondent 答题者
coding system 编码系统
quantify 量化

◇Leading questions—They **inject** interviewer bias.

◇Compound questions—They may generate a partial or non-response.

◇Judging questions—They can lead to guarded or partial responses.

◇Ambiguous or vague questions—They produce meaningless responses.

◇**Acronyms** and **jargon**—These may be unknown to the respondents.

◇Double negatives—They may create misunderstanding.

◇Long surveys—They discourage respondents' participation.

Step 9: Design the data analysis and reporting format. As a final check on the instrument, build the tables and charts, and fill them with test data. Ask the question, "If these tables and charts are filled in, will I be able to make the decisions I've planned?" Other useful questions to address include:

◇What type of analysis will I need to perform? How simple or **sophisticated** should it be?

◇Who will analyze the data? How long will it take?

◇For automated analysis, what format must the survey results use?

You may need to **iterate** between steps 8 and 9 to ensure you will have the data needed to meet your survey needs.

(3) Finalizing survey logistics.（合理组织调查工作）

Step 10: Determine sample size and selection. Sample size is driven by many factors, including: the survey type you have chosen, the complexity and relative **homogeneity** of your target audience, and the **margin** of error you and your users are willing to **tolerate** in this survey. The selection of the sample size grows in importance as the audience size and diversity increase, and as the importance of the decisions made from this information increases. Sometimes users of the survey information will want you to assure them that you have sampled adequately from certain groups they care about. Answering the following questions will clarify your sample size:

◇How many completed surveys do I need?

**单词注释**

inject 引入
acronym 缩写字
jargon 行话
sophisticated 复杂的
iterate 重复
homogeneity 一致性
margin 极限
tolerate 忍受

◇How many people must be involved in order to get the needed number of completed surveys?

◇How will we reach them?

Large samples are not necessary for many surveys. A sample of 40 to 50 surveys is often quite adequate, and 100 **suffices** in most cases. At this point in the process you should consult a survey expert to assure that your approach is well-grounded. You may need to iterate between steps 6 and 10 to ensure you are reaching the right number of desired respondents.

Step 11: Determine data-entry methods. Once survey data are collected, ensure that the data are accurately recorded so they are ready for analysis. Questions to ask include the following:

◇Who will perform the data entry?

◇How much time will it take?

◇Will we use a spreadsheet program, a database program or a survey-analysis software program?

◇How will we assure data quality and accuracy?

Specific design tools are available to increase the ease and accuracy of data entry. Consult a survey specialist for ideas.

Step 12: Pre-testing the survey. Before distributing a survey to your customers, always pretest the survey. No matter how confident you are in the survey design, pre-testing will help you:

◇Determine whether your instructions are understood.

◇Identify questions that may be misunderstood or that are poorly worded.

◇Determine whether rating scales are understood.

◇Determine how long it will take your customers to complete the survey.

◇Determine the customers' overall level of interest in completing the survey.

One method to pretest your survey is through a **pilot** group process. Pilot group participants should be representative members of your survey's target audience. The pretest should be administered in person, with participants understanding their role.

You will want to look for questions not answered, several

单词注释

suffice 足够
pilot 先行的

responses given for the same question and comments written in the **margins**. All are signals that the question may not have been understood and may need revision.

You should conduct follow-up group discussions with your survey team to gain additional insight into the strengths and weaknesses of your survey product and to identify suggested improvements.

单词注释

margin 页边空白

※ A Sample for Assignment 3

| **Mini-Swallow Grocery** | | | | | |
|---|---|---|---|---|---|
| **Customer Survey**<br>Mini-Swallow Grocery is committed to customer satisfaction and would like to know how well we're doing. Your answers will help us to identify areas needing improvement. If you have questions about this survey, please contact Henry Zhang (0750-3725208). Thank you for your time and comments. | | | | | |
| What is your overall satisfaction with Mini-Swallow Grocery? | | | | | |
| | 5 (Very satisfied) | 4 | 3 | 2 | 1 (Very dissatisfied) |
| | ☐ | ☐ | ☐ | ☐ | ☐ |
| How satisfied are you with the following areas? | | | | | |
| | 5 (Very satisfied) | 4 | 3 | 2 | 1 (Very dissatisfied) |
| The space | ☐ | ☐ | ☐ | ☐ | ☐ |
| The price | ☐ | ☐ | ☐ | ☐ | ☐ |
| Business hours | ☐ | ☐ | ☐ | ☐ | ☐ |
| Ability to meet customers' needs | ☐ | ☐ | ☐ | ☐ | ☐ |
| How satisfied are you with the environment of Mini-Swallow Grocery? | | | | | |
| | 5 (Very satisfied) | 4 | 3 | 2 | 1 (Very dissatisfied) |
| The lighting | ☐ | ☐ | ☐ | ☐ | ☐ |
| The color of the wall | ☐ | ☐ | ☐ | ☐ | ☐ |
| The ventilation | ☐ | ☐ | ☐ | ☐ | ☐ |
| The inner decoration | ☐ | ☐ | ☐ | ☐ | ☐ |
| The outer look | ☐ | ☐ | ☐ | ☐ | ☐ |

(continued)

| | |
|---|---|
| Compared with the alternative services, our services are: | |
| □ | Much better. |
| □ | Somewhat better. |
| □ | About the same. |
| □ | Somewhat worse. |
| □ | Much worse. |
| What do you think of the staff? | |
| □ | Kind enough. |
| □ | Not so kind. |
| □ | Very experienced. |
| □ | Need to be trained. |
| How often do you visit Mini-Swallow Grocery? | |
| □ | Daily. |
| □ | Once a week or more. |
| □ | Several times a year. |
| □ | Once a year. |
| □ | Other: ______________ |
| What do you suggest us to do urgently to improve our service? | |
| □ | Expand the store. |
| □ | Hire more skilled shop assistants. |
| □ | Remodel the store. |
| □ | Get more items to sell. |
| □ | Add after-sales services. |
| Do you agree or disagree with the following statements? | |
| □ | The window displays are appealing. |
| □ | The store is well **laid out**. |
| □ | The **signage** is clear. |
| □ | The signage is **informative**. |
| □ | The store is clean and tidy. |
| □ | The store has a pleasant shopping **atmosphere**. |
| □ | The store is easy to move about in. |
| □ | There are sufficient **checkouts**. |

**单词注释**

lay out 设计，布置，布局
signage 标志
informative 信息丰富的
atmosphere 气氛
checkout 付款处，收银台

### Your Assignment 3

Survey planning can be completed quickly and without a lot of formality. Doing your homework will ensure the most useful survey results at the lowest cost. Survey goals and objectives are the key to the entire effort. Writing the questions is a very important and visible element in your survey.

To have a successful survey, you should concentrate on the planning and design, and let the steps we've offered lead you to the necessary questions and format. You can bring in and **collaborate** with experts as you need them to help you produce a quality product.

## Stage 5 SWOT Analysis 强弱机危分析

SWOT analysis is an extremely useful tool for understanding and decision-making for all sorts of situations in business and organizations. SWOT is an acronym for strengths, weaknesses, opportunities, and threats. Information about the origins and inventors of SWOT analysis is below. SWOT analysis headings provide a good framework for reviewing strategy, position and direction of a company or business proposition, or any other idea. Completing a SWOT analysis is very simple, and is a good subject for workshop **sessions**. SWOT analysis also works well in **brainstorming** meetings. SWOT analysis is used for business planning, strategic planning, competitor evaluation, marketing, business and product development and research reports. You can also use SWOT analysis exercises for team building games.

SWOT analysis provides a structure for analyzing either your own strengths and weaknesses, and the opportunities and threats you face, or in a work context for analyzing the strengths, weaknesses, opportunities and threats a business or event faces. Ideally, it is one step in a process which helps you to:

◇Appreciate the strengths of a situation, and you may then

**单词注释**

collaborate 协作
session 会议，会期，
brainstorming 头脑风暴

decide to build on them.

◇Define the weaknesses, which you might choose to **minimize**.

◇Make the most of the opportunities that present themselves, and recognize the possible threats and treat them in a planned and organized way.

SWOT analysis is not an end in itself but a step before some action planning. It usually benefits from discussion, and other people's perspectives. Remember to be realistic and focused on what really happens.

In a SWOT analysis you want to note issues under the four headings. If you are new to the process, the following questions may be helpful prompts to your thinking:

(1) Strengths. (优势)

◇What are your **assets** (buildings, equipments and other facilities)?

◇What does the company do well (in sales, marketing, operations, management)?

◇What do other people see as your strengths?

◇Where does the organization compete well?

For example:

◇There are no other shops nearby selling the same things as you do.

◇You have a very good reputation for selling high quality goods.

◇You can offer very good price.

◇Your products are of better quality.

◇Your workers or staff are professional in selling this kind of goods.

◇Your shop stands near the center of the city, where there are a great number of potential customers coming and going every day.

(2) Weaknesses. (劣势)

◇What can be developed?

◇What could you improve?

**单词注释**

minimize 最小化
asset 财产

◇What is working less **optimally** than you wish?

◇What is being done badly?

◇What is the competition doing better?

◇What should you avoid doing?

For example:

◇Your shop is very small and there is no room to keep more goods in stock.

◇You are not making enough money to employ an assistant, so you cannot keep the shop open as long as you would like.

◇Your product may not be attractive enough for people to buy.

◇Your prices are higher than others.

◇The location is far away from the city center.

(3) Opportunities.(机遇)

◇If there were no **constraints** what would you like to do?

◇What might be possible?

◇What will happen in the next few years?

◇Where do you/your organization want to be in five years?

◇Who might you want to work with?

◇What could be a win-win situation?

◇How may new technologies change your practices?

◇What financial/governmental/**legislative** changes can benefit you in the near future?

For example:

◇There is a larger shop in the next door building and it is unoccupied at present.

◇The school nearby is going to expand, so there will be more students who might become your customers.

◇ There are more and more buildings to be built in two years, which means there will be more and more residents who need what you can offer.

◇ The government wants to accelerate development of this city.

(4) Threats.(危机)

◇What are the barriers to your development?

单词注释

optimally 最佳地
constraint 约束
legislative 立法的

◇What sort of **obstacles** do you face?

◇Who else might move in and take over your tasks/job/business?

◇What are **rival** organizations doing?

◇What are your competitors doing that may result in a loss of your clients, customers, and market share?

◇Is the changing technology threatening your position?

◇Will new technologies/developments change you roles?

◇What change is coming?

For example:

◇You have heard that the owners of your present building want to **demolish** it to build new offices.

◇A competitor is planning to open a shop like yours just around the corner.

◇Some of your staff are not so experienced and often cause troubles with the customers.

◇It is very hard to apply for a loan needed to set up your company.

◇No proper or right market can be found.

◇More and more people tend to shop online.

※A Sample for Assignment 4

**SWOT Analysis**

Strengths:

◇The management of Mini-Swallow Grocery is given the **exclusive right** to run an on-campus groceries store.

◇The store serves the students and teachers who need stationery for their study and work.

◇The store has extensive contact with the students and teachers, who provide information on the goods needed.

◇The store purchases directly from manufacturers, so it can offer larger discounts to the customers.

◇The rent of the store is not so high. This allows the store to lower the prices.

单词注释

obstacle 障碍
rival 竞争的；敌对的
demolish 毁坏；粉碎
exclusive right 专有权

Weaknesses:

◇The narrow space constrains the store from increasing stock and from offering more services. Customers often do not have much choice when choosing items they want urgently.

◇It is impossible to expand the store at the present location, because the rooms around are all being occupied by the cafeteria that refuses to give any up.

◇The college did not have a plan to build a grocery store in the original place. Therefore, it is difficult to find an ideal site for the new store. It may end up in some building far from the center of the campus.

◇The manager, who used to work in a hotel, lacks experience of running a grocery.

Opportunities:

◇There are eight schools in this area, but there is no **decent** grocery store around.

◇There are more than ten thousand students and six hundred teachers and staff living in the campus.

◇The number of students at the college is growing rapidly due to the fact that the Chinese government is encouraging universities to enlarge their enrollment to satisfy the people's demand for higher education.

◇There are a great number of local residents and workers from many a factory nearby.

◇China has already joined the WTO and need **qualified personnel** to deal with the relevant issues as China becomes more **integrated** into the world community. The university has excellent programs to train such candidates.

◇It is difficult to find a place to make photocopies or print a document from a computer disk, especially in the evenings.

Threats:

◇A competitor is planning to open a supermarket just around the corner outside the college.

◇The shop assistants are not so experienced and kind, which often makes customers unsatisfied.

◇Goods prices are getting higher and higher recently. So it is getting more and more difficult to offer larger discount to our customers.

◇Online shops that offer **discount** goods are attracting more and more customers.

**单词注释**

decent 得体的；像样的
qualified personnel 人才
integrated 完整的；互相协调的
discount 折扣

### Your Assignment 4

Now write a SWOT analysis for the business you have chosen. To do this, use all the information you have prepared so far. This includes:

◇What you really know about the business and its location, competitors, etc.

◇Your estimate of its financial situation.

◇The information contained in your customer profile and the ideas in your focus group report.

◇Anything else that you think is a realistic **assessment** of the context for the business.

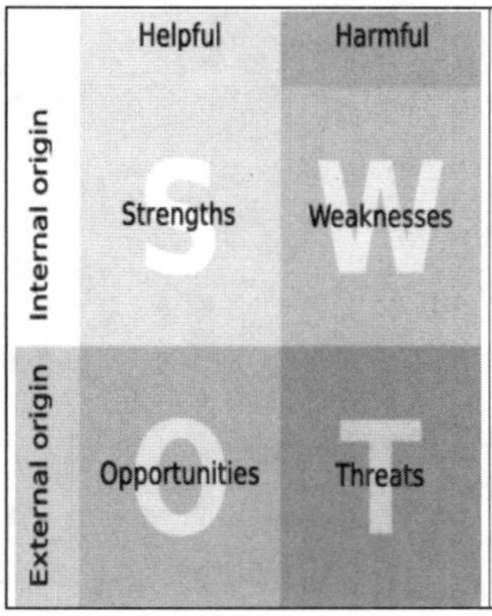


***Note**: Here comes the time when you show your tutor everything you have done while carrying out the tasks 1, 2, 3 and 4; you should also give him or her copies of the four tasks that are to be assessed.

Task 1: business analysis

Task 2: the customer profile and the focus group report

Task 3: the customer survey design

Task 4: the SWOT analysis

单词注释

assessment 估价，评估

highlight 强调

## Stage 6&7 Action Plan & Activity Flow Chart 项目实施计划及流程图

After gathering all the information about the business, and deciding on the objectives of our project, we have now reached the stage when we can plan in detail all the things we will have to do to reach those objectives. In other words, we need to plan the activities.

### (1) Critical Path Analysis.（关键路径分析）

The critical path analysis is a tool that illustrates the individual tasks of a project **highlighting** the expected starting and finishing tasks of each. More precisely, the critical path analysis can be used to:

◇Estimate the minimum/maximum time that tasks will be started and completed.

◇Estimate the minimum time that the whole project will take.

◇Identify if resources are not being used effectively.

◇Be aware that any tasks that may cause a possible delay.

Ultimately, the critical path analysis will suggest which tasks are critical to keep on time and **anticipate** that the delay in any one of the tasks will delay the whole project.

The critical path analysis is hard to explain in more detail without the use of **diagrams**, so the working example in the following section will make it all clearer.

Example:

ABC Limited has decided to carry out some research to ultimately create a selling strategy for their new product. They have decided to create a **questionnaire**, which they will issue to the public personally. In addition, they will use a mail **shot** to send out a similar survey to get the opinions of those that live outside of the area.

Each task (A – G) has been given an expected completion time (in weeks). Time is crucial for ABC Limited and the manager has requested a critical path analysis of the project as shown.

| Task | Description | Order/Logic | Time |
|---|---|---|---|
| A | Plan primary research | To be completed first | 1 wk |
| B | Prepare mail shot (postal survey) | Start when A is completed | 3 wks |
| C | Prepare questionnaire | Start when A is completed | 2 wks |
| D | Send and wait for mail shot replies | Start when B is completed | 3 wks |
| E | Issue questionnaire | Start when C is completed | 3 wks |
| F | Compile and analyze results | Start when D & E is completed | 2 wks |
| G | Plan selling campaign | Start when D–F is completed | 2 wks |

Now, take a good look at the diagram below. Each circle (**node**) will be used to enter specific data. The numbers currently

**单词注释**

anticipate 预计
diagram 图表
questionnaire 问卷调查
shot 发出
node 结点

in the nodes (1 – 7) are only there to make following the diagram easier—nothing more. The arrows represent the tasks and each is given their respective completion times.

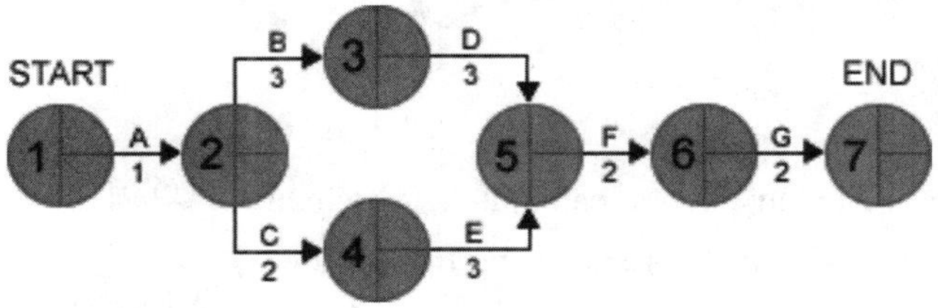


Before we move on, look at the above table again and ensure that you understand what is being said by linking it back to the diagram. Basically, all tasks cannot start until the previous task has been completed. This is not true for tasks B and C which can start at the same time—this is the only **tricky** area.

Firstly, we have to identify the earliest starting time (EST) for each task. This figure then enter into the top right hand segment of the node. To work out the EST, we move from left to right on the diagram. The diagram below shows all the EST for the project and by **hovering** the mouse over a node, it will show how this figure was obtained.

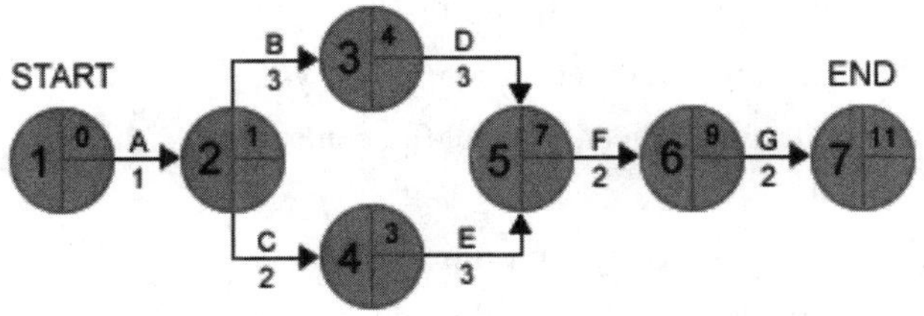


Secondly, we have to work out the latest finish time (LFT) for each task. This is worked out similar to the EST except we subtract figures and work from right to left on the diagram. The LFT is then placed inside the bottom right hand segment of the node.

Ignore the **bold line** for now, it will be explained later. Remember: from right to left.

单词注释

tricky 棘手的
hover 悬停
bold line 粗线

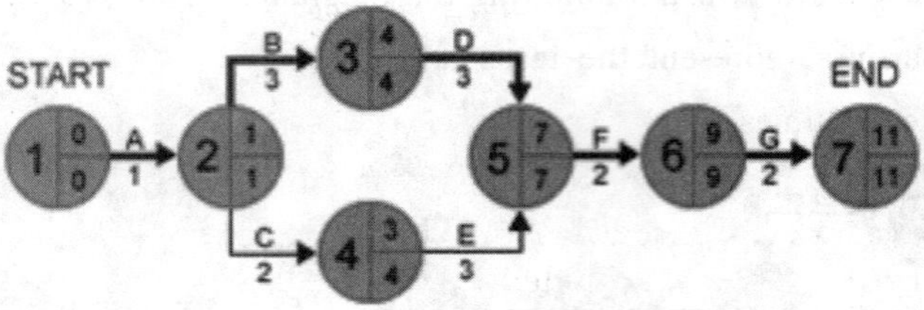


Now the EST and the LFT have been calculated, we can determine the critical path. This is found by recognizing those nodes where the EST = LFT.

By looking at the above diagram, all the nodes have equal EST and LFT except for number 4. By acknowledging this, we can identify the critical path as: A – B – D – F – G (highlighted by the bold line)

In other words, there must be no delays in completing these tasks, otherwise the project completion time will be delayed beyond the expected 11 weeks. This is impracticable for the tasks that do not lie on the critical path.

(2) Gantt Charts.（甘特图）

It is necessary that you know about Gantt charts as you may well come across them in your further studies or in business. Producing a Gantt chart, however, requires special computer software, so you won't be asked to produce one for your own project. Just get the general idea about it. That'll be quite enough.

According to **Wikipedia**, the free **encyclopedia**, a Gantt chart is a type of bar chart that illustrates a project schedule. Gantt charts illustrate the start and finish dates of the terminal elements and summary elements of a project. Terminal elements and summary elements **comprise** the work **breakdown** structure of the project. Some Gantt charts also show the **dependency** (i.e. **precedence** network) relationships between activities.

This chart can be used to show the activities in detail, not only the information we have used so far, but also how much **variation** in time is possible for each activity without creating problems to the project.

It can also show the links between activities and can be

**单词注释**

Wikipedia 维基百科
encyclopedia 百科全书
comprise 包括，包含
breakdown 崩溃，故障
dependency 从属关系
precedence 优先
variation 变动

updated regularly. Every time you make a change, the chart adjusts everything else to fit.

### ※A Sample for Assignment 5

### Action Plan

The project will take 8 weeks to implement after it is approved.

| Task | Description | Order/Logic | Time |
|---|---|---|---|
| A | Identify and negotiate the rental of the new premises.<br>Sign the contract with the college. | To be completed first. | Week 1 |
| B | Design the new store **layout**.<br>Prepare for remodeling of the new store. | Start when A is completed. | Week 2 |
| C | Start remodeling the store.<br>Order new shelves, equipment and furniture and new goods.<br>Hire new shop assistants. | Start when B is completed. | Week 3 |
| D | Start training the new shop assistants. | Start when C is completed. | Week 4 |
| E | Check and accept the remodeling project.<br>**Publicize** on campus store expansion. | Start when D is completed. | Week 5 |
| F | Get new equipment delivered and installed.<br>Clean the new store and pack up stock in the old store. | Start when E is completed. | Week 6 |
| G | Close the present store and move everything to the new store.<br>Put the old stock on the shelves.<br>Get the new stock delivered and put on the shelves. | Start when F is completed. | Week 7 |
| H | Hold the opening **ceremony**. | Start when G is completed. | Week 8 |

**单词注释**

layout 布局，安排，设计
publicize 宣传；公布
ceremony 仪式

## ※A Sample for Assignment 6

**Activity Flow Chart**

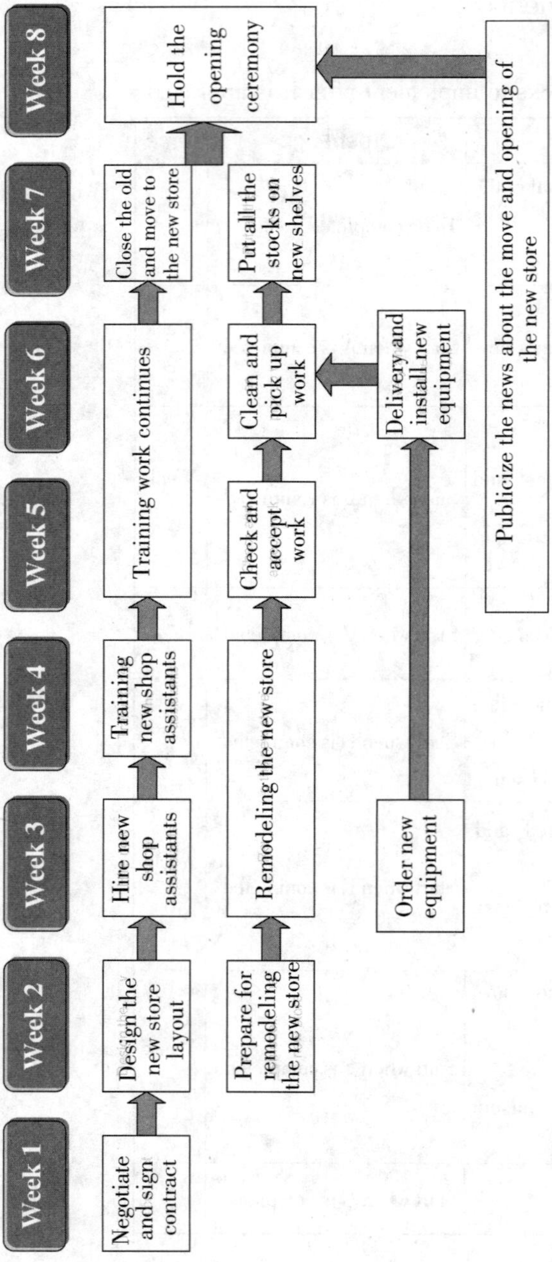

### Your Assignment 5 and 6

More hints for you here:

◇Clearly list all the things that will have to be done in order to carry out your business project. To do this, you are suggested to list everything in a table in a logical sequence at the beginning: What has to be done first, then what, and how?

◇Put each set of tasks as a simple flow chart, with each task in a separate box. Do it directly on paper at this stage.

◇Looking at your flow charts, decide which tasks MUST be done first and which can be done independently. Now **combine** your flow charts into a single one.

◇Work out how long each task will take. This will enable you to work out how long the project will take.

◇Try to start from the end of the project and work backwards, you can decide when each activity will take place.

◇Add these times to your flow chart, and you should produce a chart like the one in the above sample.

◇You are required to use Microsoft Word to complete the chart. Don't use other software. Make sure you identify the critical path by using different **arrows**.

◇Don't just make a copy of the sample given. Yours should be different from it.

## Stage 8 Cost Breakdown 成本核算

All manufacturing companies sell their products to make profit. The profit on each product sold can be defined as the difference between the selling price of the product and the total cost of making the product. Cost, therefore, plays a very important role in the product design process. To be successful, a product must not only satisfy a set of **functions** defined in the product design **specification**, but also be possible to build the product within the cost **criteria** set out at the start of the project. Before the development of any product

**单词注释**

combine 组合
arrow 箭头
function 功能，作用
specification 规格；规范
criterion（*pl.* -ria）标准

begins, it is essential to perform some forms of economic analysis on the product to determine if it is worth making. This may involve some forms of market analysis to determine what the customer is willing to pay for a product.

The costs involved in any product can be spilt into development costs and the product cost. Interestingly, some companies do not actually know what their costs are, which leaves them open to the possibility that their actual costs may be more than the selling price of their product! An example of this was the Mini when it was first produced in the early 1960's. Market research suggested that the car should be sold for less than £500 so the company priced the car at £499. Later when they analyzed the cost of producing the car they found that the car cost around £530 to build, resulting in large losses for the manufacturer.

As for the project we are doing here, the costing should consist of the following 4 aspects:

(1) Costs of materials and equipment.(材料与设备成本)

If your project involves **redecorating** your store, you would include here the costs of the paint and the paint brushes, and some other materials necessary for the redecoration.

Meanwhile, it might include the cost of renting any equipment which you don't want to buy and keep, such as a **ladder** to reach the **ceiling**. In a different project you might have to include the costs of things like postage, telephone charges, network, etc.

(2) Costs of labor.(劳务成本)

Generally speaking, total labor costs are the sum of wages and salaries (pay) paid by an employer to an employee, plus any other costs **incurred** by the employer. As well as wages and salaries, total labor costs include employer's social **contributions** (including national insurance, contributions and **pensions**, paid on behalf of the employee) and other non-wage costs including sickness, **maternity** and **paternity** costs, vocational training costs, recruitment costs and benefits in kind. The latter include company

**单词注释**

redecorate 重新装饰
ladder 梯子
ceiling 天花板
incur 招致，引起
contribution 贡献；成就
pension 津贴
maternity 产期
paternity 陪产期

cars, mobile phones and **accommodation**.

(3) Costs of finance.(财务成本)

These costs might include the interest you will pay the bank if you have to borrow money to carry out the project. They might also include the value of any earnings that you may lose in order to carry out the project. So if you cannot do your own job while your office is being repainted, you would have to include the amount of money you would earn if you didn't stop working for that time.

(4) Contingency allowance.(应急费用)

A contingency allowance is for additional unforeseen elements of cost within the defined project scope. It is particularly important because previous experience relating estimates and actual costs has shown that unforeseen events which will increase costs are likely to occur. If an allowance for **escalation** is included in the contingency, it should be regarded as a separate item, determined to fit expected escalation conditions of the project. For example, if you had estimated that the painter would need two days to do his job, but the job turned out to be more complicated than expected and it actually took three days, you would have to find the money to pay him for an extra day. Contingency costs are usually estimated as a percentage of the total of all the other costs. Depending on how complex the project is, you might use 5%, 10% or even 15% as the figure to put into your costing. Using the risk analysis will help you decide how much you need to allow for contingencies.

单词注释

accommodation 住宿
contingency 意外事件
escalation 扩大，增加

※A Sample for Assignment 7

Listed below is the cost breakdown for the Mini-Swallow Grocery expansion project as requested:

| Item | Description | Quantity Unit | Unit | Unit Price | Total Cost |
|---|---|---|---|---|---|
| Rental cost | The new **premises** would cost no less than RMB55,000.00 to rent per year as shown in the following: | | | | |
| | Rental cost | | | **Lump sum** | ¥ 55, 000.00 |
| Remodeling | The remodeling costs for the new store would be RMB127,700 as shown in the following: | | | | |
| 1 | Labor cost | | | Lump sum | ¥ 75, 000.00 |
| 2 | Windows | 10 | set | ¥ 800.00 | ¥ 8, 000.00 |
| 3 | Flooring | 8,000 | $m^2$ | ¥ 1.00 | ¥ 8, 000.00 |
| 4 | Paint | 500 | kg | ¥ 12.00 | ¥ 6, 000.00 |
| 5 | Ceiling | 700 | $m^2$ | ¥ 10.00 | ¥ 7, 000.00 |
| 6 | Lumber | | | Lump sum | ¥ 4, 500.00 |
| 7 | Lighting | | | Lump sum | ¥ 15, 000.00 |
| 8 | **Glue and tools** | | | Lump sum | ¥ 1, 200.00 |
| 9 | **Cement and putty** | 6 | ton | Lump sum | ¥ 3, 000.00 |
| | | | | Sub-total: | ¥127, 700.00 |
| Equipment | The cost of equipment in the new bookshop would be RMB70, 300 as shown in the following: | | | | |
| 1 | Photocopier | 1 | set | ¥ 35,000.00 | ¥ 35, 000.00 |
| 2 | Shelves | 500 | set | ¥ 30.00 | ¥ 15, 000.00 |
| 3 | Office furniture | 1 | set | ¥ 3, 000.00 | ¥ 3, 000.00 |
| 4 | Computers | 2 | set | ¥ 4, 500.00 | ¥ 9, 000.00 |
| 5 | Printers | 2 | set | ¥ 1, 500.00 | ¥ 3, 000.00 |
| 6 | Air conditioners | 2 | set | ¥ 2, 000.00 | ¥ 4, 000.00 |
| 7 | Armchairs | 3 | set | ¥ 100.00 | ¥ 300.00 |
| 8 | Office supplies | 1 | set | ¥ 1, 000.00 | ¥ 1, 000.00 |
| | | | | Sub-total: | ¥ 70, 300.00 |

(continued)

**单词注释**

premise 生产经营场所
lump sum 整数
glue 胶水
tool 工具
cement 水泥
putty 油灰

| Budget | The annual increase in the operating budget would be RMB35, 300 as shown in the following: | | | | |
|---|---|---|---|---|---|
| 1 | Wages | | | Lump sum | ¥ 28, 000.00 |
| 2 | **Utilities** | | | Lump sum | ¥ 3, 000.00 |
| 3 | Equipment maintenance | | | Lump sum | ¥ 1, 500.00 |
| 4 | Consultants fee | | | Lump sum | ¥ 2, 800.00 |
| | | | | Sub-total: | ¥ 35, 300.00 |
| Total cost of the whole project = Initial costs + Recurrent costs = RMB288, 300 as shown in the following: | | | | | |
| Intial costs | Remodeling | | | Lump sum | ¥ 127, 700.00 |
| | Equipment | | | Lump sum | ¥ 70, 300.00 |
| | | | | Sub-total: | ¥ 198, 000.00 |
| Recurrent costs | Rental | | | Lump sum | ¥ 55, 000.00 |
| | Operating budget | | | Lump sum | ¥ 35,300.00 |
| | | | | Sub-total: | ¥ 90, 300.00 |
| | | | | Total: | ¥ 288, 300.00 |

单词注释

utility 公共设施
refurbishment 翻新

## Your Assignment 7

It's your turn to make an itemized list of the costs of everything that will be needed to carry out your project.

All the costs that are directly related to the project should be included, except the ordinary costs which you have to pay for even if there is no project.

Consider your costs under the following headings, though not all may be relevant to your particular project.

- premises, **refurbishment** and furniture
- equipment
- services
- staff
- contingency

Figure out totals for each category and then an overall total. Try to get it done after the sample given.

## Stage 8 Risk Analysis 风险分析

### (1) Risk analysis overview.(风险分析概述)

Risk analysis is the systematic study of uncertainties and risks we **encounter** in business, engineering, public policy and many other areas. Risk analysis seek to identify the risks faced by an institution or a business unit, understand how and when they arise, and estimate the impact (financial or otherwise) of adverse outcomes. Risk managers start with risk analysis, then seek to take actions that will **mitigate** or **hedge** these risks.

Some institutions, such as banks and investment management firms, are in the business of taking risks every day. Risk analysis and management are clearly crucial for these institutions. One of the roles of risk management in these firms is to quantify the financial risks involved in each investment, trading, or other business activity, and **allocate** a risk budget across these activities. Banks in particular are required by their **regulators** to identify and quantify their risks, often computing measures such as value at risk (VaR), and ensure that they have adequate capital to maintain **solvency** should the worst (or near-worst) outcomes occur.

### (2) The process of risk analysis.(风险分析步骤)

The process of risk analysis includes identifying and quantifying uncertainties, estimating their impact on outcomes that we care about, building a risk analysis model that expresses these elements in quantitative form, exploring the model through **simulation** and sensitivity analysis, and making risk management decisions that can help us avoid, mitigate, or otherwise deal with risk.

### (3) Identify and quantify uncertainty.(找出并量化不确定因素)

In risk analysis, our goal is to identify each important source of uncertainty, and quantify its **magnitude** as well as we can. For example, we may not know our competitor's exact price, but we can place **bounds** on it, based on known production and marketing costs.

**单词注释**

encounter 遇到
mitigate 使缓和，使温和
hedge 防止
allocate 分派，分配
regulator 监管人员
solvency 偿付能力
simulation 模拟，模仿
magnitude 重要性
bound 范围

While we can't predict the exact number of people shopping at a store each day, we can examine past data for the frequency of days when (say) 10, 20, 30, …, 100 people shopped, and use it to estimate a distribution of shoppers on future days. This process of identifying and quantifying uncertainties is a key step in risk analysis.

**(4) Compute the impact of uncertainty.（预估不确定因素的影响）**

Our next step is to accurately estimate the impact of the uncertainties on the outcomes we care about. For example, we may not be able to predict demand for our product exactly; but given a number for demand, since we know our costs and margins, we can often calculate the impact on our net profit. We may not know the exact number of shoppers on any future day; but given a number of shoppers, we can calculate how many people we need to serve, and estimate the sales we're likely to generate.

**(5) Stakeholder analysis.（利益相关者分析）**

Stakeholder analysis is a form of analysis that aims to identify the stakeholders that are likely to be affected by the activities and outcomes of a project, and to assess how those stakeholders are likely to be impacted by the project. Stakeholder analysis has the goal of developing cooperation between the stakeholder and the project team and, ultimately, assuring successful outcomes for the project.

A stakeholder analysis is performed when there is a need to clarify the **consequences** of **envisaged** changes, or at the start of new projects and in connection with organizational changes generally.

It is important to identify all stakeholders for the purpose of identifying their success criteria and turning these into quality goals. For example, one of the stakeholders in a redecoration project might be the painter who actually does the work. Obviously, if he falls sick and cannot do his work, your project might be delayed quite seriously, so you have to ask yourself if there is a real risk of this happening. If he is an old man who works alone for himself in winter, you might think it a real possibility. You would then have

**单词注释**

stakeholder 利益相关者
consequence 结果
envisage 设想

to plan what you would do if he does in fact fall sick. If, however, he is just an employee of a decorating company, you might **assume** that there is no risk to your project because the company would have to send someone else to replace him.

The stakeholders in the project to put new shelves in your shop might be the manufacturers and suppliers of the new shelves. What is the risk that they might be late in delivering the shelves to you? If you think that there is a real risk which might happen and that it would cause a delay in re-opening the shop for a week, you need to plan what to do if it does happen. Or you might decide to avoid the risk by using a different supplier who you know will be more reliable.

You need to look for risks in three main areas as shown in the following table:

| | |
|---|---|
| A | People related:<br>Will people do what they are supposed to do?<br>Is there anyone who might cause real problems to the project?<br>Will people be able to do things in the time allowed? |
| B | Time related:<br>Are there any parts of the project where a delay will cause serious problems for the project? |
| C | Product related:<br>Will things supplied to the project be exactly what you want?<br>Is there a danger that there might be faults in the equipment needed for the project?<br>Will everything you want be available? |

### (6) Disruption to your existing business.(对经营现状的影响)

Eventually, do remember to consider whether your existing business or work might suffer from carrying out the project and what the effects would be. Since the effects might be quite serious,

单词注释

assume 假定，设想
disruption 中断

you should have to plan ahead of time to cope with them.

Suppose you have to close your store temporarily for a week or so in order to get it remodeled, which means you will lose money because you won't sell things as you usually do. You will need to allow for this in the costing for your project. This is lost revenue.

In addition, to lost revenue, there may be some other additional costs. For example, you may still have to pay your employees even if they don't work while the store is closed. Alternatively, if you stop employing them and plan to recruit new staff once the project is completed, you will have to allow for the additional costs of recruiting and training the new staff.

In another situation your business might be one that you could carry on doing in temporary premises. In this case, you wouldn't lose revenue but have to allow for the extra cost of renting the temporary premises.

All these things may result in impacts on the cost of your project, so you should now go back and if necessary, **revise** your costing to **take account of** the results of your risk analysis.

Now look at the case study to see what a risk analysis is and what impacts it has on the project costing. You will also see examples of suggestions for managing the risks identified.

**单词注释**

revise 修改
take account of 顾及
fall into 分成

## ※A Sample for Assignment 8

### Risk Analysis

Before putting the plan into practice, the management finds that the following problems might affect the successful completion of the project. These problems, also called risks, generally **fall into** three categories:

(1) **People-related.**

◇The new employees may not be good at selling at all.

◇Some dishonest students may pilfer from the store.

◇The clerks next door may not be happy with the noises resulting from the remodeling of the new site and may demand no remodeling during the working hours.

(2) **Time-related**.

◇The university may shorten the period of the **lease** of the new site and even worse, **expropriate** the new store.

◇The loan may not be obtained from the bank in time, so the workers may not be paid on time, which may cause the delay of this project.

◇The newly ordered shelves may not arrive in time, causing delay in the opening of the new store.

◇The weather may turn to be bad, which may slow down the speed of remodeling.

(3) **Product-related**.

◇The supply channels may be blocked, which may result in the rise of prices.

◇The paint applied to the walls may not **live up to** the quality and begin to **fall off** shortly after the decoration.

◇The new stock may not cater to the interests of the customer.

Since it's impossible to **eradicate** all these risks, the store manager has to control and manage them. Here are three measures to be taken:

◇Carry out a market research. In order to prevent the dangers from happening, we'll carry out a market research among our target customers so that we can improve the popularity of the stock and remain constant contact with the instructors to get the latest information of products and the market.

◇Be ready to deal with urgency. Prepare alternatives beforehand in case the dangers actually happen. We will keep contacting more clerk candidates as **substitutes** in case the employed are not qualified. What's more, try our best to finish the remodeling within the weekends if the dissatisfaction occurred from the neighboring clerks.

◇Set aside a certain percentage of the total budget as contingency allowance to take account of the unexpected risks, such as to **cover** the **pilferage** loss and to cover the re-painting expense.

After the risk analysis, we think three more items should be added to the total costs:

| | |
|---|---|
| Public relations | 2,000 yuan per annum |
| Market research | 1,000 yuan per annum |
| Contingency allowance | 1% of the annual profit |

**单词注释**

lease 租约
expropriate 征用
live up to 符合
fall off 脱落
eradicate 杜绝
substitute 代替者，代用品
cover 投保
pilferage 偷窃

So the total cost of the project would be:

RMB288,300 + 5, 000 + 1% of the annual profit.

That is about RMB300,000.

### Your Assignment 8

#### (1) Stakeholder analysis.

List all the people who are, or might be, concerned with or affected by the project. Make a note of what their interests and concerns might be.

Now consider whether any of them might be the cause of problems that would delay the project or might make it unsuccessful.

Think also whether there are other risks to the project that you need to be aware of.

#### (2) Risk analysis and management plan.

You should now write down a statement of what you think might be serious risks to the success of the project.

After finishing that, add a section showing what you propose to do to avoid the risks, or what actions you will take if any of them actually happen.

#### (3) Revise your costing.

Some of the things that you have listed in the risk management plan may add extra costs to your project, so you should now go back to your costing and revise it as necessary.

# Chapter Four

# 第四章

## A Business Proposal

## 商务项目计划书

# Chapter Four

## A Business Proposal

| 单词注释 |
|---|
| fierce 激烈的，残忍的 |
| aggressive 进取的 |
| award 授予，给予 |
| joint venture 合资企业 |
| entity 实体 |
| tender 投标 |
| bidder 投标人 |
| stand 立足于 |
| submission 意见，看法 |
| alliance 联盟 |

### 1. The General Idea about Business Proposals 商务项目计划书的基本概念

A business proposal is a document that persuades the reader of it to follow a plan or course of action. The plan may offer a change or an improvement within an organization or to provide specific goods or services to a potential buyer (John Hilton, 2002).

It is said that business in the 1990s means **fierce** competition, **aggressive** marketing and strategic alliances. The extent to which a business succeeds or fails often depends upon that business's ability to be **awarded** contracts or to attract other businesses into **joint ventures** or strategic alliances. To accomplish either one usually requires two key factors: good ideas and the ability to present those good ideas in a superbly developed business proposal.

In general, business proposals are developed for one or two possible reasons.

A business **entity** calls for **tenders** or invites you to submit a RFP (Request for Proposal). In this case, your goal is to be "short listed", meaning that you will be one of the three or four **bidders** who is awarded an interview. Your proposal must **stand** among possibly dozens of **submissions**.

You have an idea, concept or project that you want to propose to someone with the goal of gaining support, funding or an **alliance**. In this case, there is no competitive bidding process. However, your proposal must make a favorable impression and must explain all the aspects of your proposed concepts clearly and quickly. A document that is vaguely written, difficult to understand or that presents more questions than answers will likely be **discarded** promptly.

## 2. Parts of a Business Proposal 商务项目计划书的组成部分

A proposal for a business project is called a business proposal, which is actually believed to be one of the forms of a formal report, and so which has three major parts just as a formal report often does:

- **preliminary** part
- body or text
- supplementary part

Fig. 4-1 shows the three major parts of a business proposal in general:

Fig. 4-1 Parts of a Business Proposal

| Preliminary part | Body or text | Supplementary part |
| --- | --- | --- |
| letter of **transmittal** | introduction | **bibliography** |
| title page | findings and analysis | |
| table of contents | summary, conclusions and recommendations | **appendix** |
| **executive summary** | | |

### (1) Preliminary part. (前辅文)

The preliminary part is the part of a proposal for a business project that appears at the very beginning, which provides the reader with information about the proposal body. From the figure above, we can see the preliminary part involves a letter of transmittal, a title page, a table of contents and an executive summary.

A letter of transmittal transmits the proposal to the receiver. This document **conveys** what you would say if you are giving the proposal directly to the receiver. Therefore, it is usually less formal than the proposal itself. A letter of transmittal **accompany** a

**单词注释**

discard 丢弃，抛弃
preliminary 初步的，预备的
transmittal 传送，转送
executive summary 摘要；概述
bibliography 参考书目，参考文献
appendix 附录
convey 传达
accompany 伴随

proposal to receivers outside the organization; if a proposal is going to a receiver internal, a memo of transmittal could be used instead. It is often the case to use direct order for the letter or memo of transmittal, beginning with a statement such as "Here is the proposal you asked me to prepare about..." Include a brief statement of the proposal objective, followed by a short summary of the proposal. End by thanking the receiver who requested the proposal and offering assistance if needed. Fig. 4 – 2 shows a sample memo of transmittal.

单词注释

curriculum (*pl.* -la) 课程

Fig. 4-2 A Sample Memo of Transmittal

| | |
|---|---|
| MLS Meade Legal Services<br>1100 Court Street<br>Cincinnati, OH 45201-1100 | |
| To: | Victor, Senior Vice President |
| From: | Henry Gates, Manager of Office Services |
| Date: | September 22nd, 2015 |
| Subject: | The Effect of Information Processing |
| On March 23rd, 2015, you asked me to prepare a report on the impact of information processing in selected legal offices in the United States. You also asked me to report the impact of information processing on business education **curricula** offered by NABTE institutions.<br>The completed report, which is attached, shows that information processing has had a significant effect on legal offices and on business education curricula. The report also includes recommendations for ways in which NABTE institutions can match their curricula to the needs of legal offices in their local areas.<br>Thank you for the chance to study this important issue, if you have any questions about the report, please call me at extension 9881. | |

A title page is the page that shows the proposal title; the name, title, and organization of the person to whom the proposal is written; the writer's name, title, organization and the date the report is submitted. Fig. 4 – 3 shows a sample title page. You may use the title page as the proposal cover if the proposal is short or if the proposal is for internal use. Otherwise, you are expected to use a cover that might be made of thicker paper or plastic. **Label** the cover with the proposal title and, if desired, with the writer's name and date.

Fig. 4-3 A Sample Title Page

**The Impact of Information Processing in**
**Selected Legal Offices and Nabte Institutions**

Prepared for
Victor
Senior Vice President
Meade Legal Services

Prepared by
Henry Gates
Manager of Office Services
Meade Legal Services

May 15th, 20××

A table of contents is a list of the report's content. You can prepare the table of contents after the report is written by listing the main headings shown in the report body and the page number where each heading is on. Fig. 4 - 4 shows a sample table of contents in general.

单词注释

label 标明

Fig. 4 – 4 A Sample Table of Contents

**Table of Contents**



单词注释

synopsis 摘要；概要

The executive summary, sometimes called a **synopsis** or an abstract, is a brief overview of the proposal. The purpose of the executive summary is to convey the key points of the proposal to the receiver. The executive summary is rather critical when a proposal is long and technical because it allows busy readers to grasp the main points quickly without reading the whole proposal. The following shows an example of an executive summary.

**Executive Summary**

The purpose of the study was to determine the impact that information processing has made in selected legal offices in the United States. Further, the study sought to ascertain the impact that information processing has made on business education curricula offered by selected NABTE institutions.

**Methods and procedures**

The participants for the study were information-processing specialists employed in legal offices throughout the United States and NABTE representatives from selected collegiate institutions. The legal participants were randomly selected from the Martindale-Hubbell Law Directory, 1998. The NABTE representatives were randomly selected from NABTE institutions located in or near the capital city in each state.

Each legal office participant completed a questionnaire, and each NABTE representative completed a business education questionnaire. The *t*-test, McNemar test, and Stuart-Maxwell test were used to analyze the data.

**Results and conclusions**

The results of the study revealed that **attorneys** hired high school graduates or two-year secretarial graduates who knew how to answer the telephone, operate a workstation, file documents electronically, use various computer software packages, and key straight copy at speeds of 60 to 80 words a minute. The data also revealed that, in general, the firms had not established **evaluation** standards for information-processing specialists and had not increased the number of these specialists since purchasing electronic workstations. The firms also had not increased the salaries of information-processing specialists. Further, the findings revealed that the cost of processing information in legal offices had decreased since the implementation of electronic workstations.

The responses received from the NABTE representatives revealed that business educators trained office technology and **comprehensive** business education majors to operate information-processing equipments, use software packages, and key documents at production rates. No changes were noted for teaching basic business or basic English skills.

**单词注释**

attorney 律师
evaluation 评估，评价
comprehensive 综合性的

(2) Body or text.（正文）

The body or text, which contains the actual proposal itself, consists of three major parts: the introduction; the findings and analysis; and the summary, conclusions, and recommendations.
The introduction states the purpose of the proposal. In the introduction you should state the problems that give rise to the project and the solution to them. You may also include the benefits that the project can bring about and the total estimated costs. The introduction

discusses several topics, including any or all of the following:

| | |
|---|---|
| **Authorization** | statement of who authorized the report and the time and manner of authorization |
| Statement of the problem | reasons for writing the report and the goals to be accomplished |
| Scope | information the report does and does not cover |
| Limitations | factors affecting the scope of the report, such as a limited amount of time or a limited budget |
| Definition of Terms | list of unfamiliar terms and their definitions |

**单词注释**

authorization 授权
alphabetic 按字母顺序
work cited 引用作品

The findings and analysis section of the proposal body present the findings and the supporting details and examines these results, while the summary, conclusions, and recommendations section summarizes the findings, draws conclusions, and makes recommendations.

### (3) Supplementary part.(后辅文)

A formal proposal may also contain supplementary parts that follow the proposal body, such as a bibliography or appendixes.

The bibliography is a list of sources used in preparing the report, arranged in **alphabetic** order by authors' names (called "**Works Cited**" when using MLA guidelines). A bibliography shows readers where the information in the proposal comes from and where to look for additional information.

## 3. Writing an Effective Business Proposal 撰写有效的商务项目计划书

It's no doubt that the service or product your small business offers is the best in the market. You know it and your employees know it. Now, if only all your prospective customers knew it too! Of course the best way to share the mission and capabilities of your company in a way that relates to the unique needs of your customers is to specifically map those elements out for them. One of the most effective ways to introduce yourself is by compiling informative and attractive business proposals.

Proposals also help you explain financial terms and procedures to your prospective customers to avoid misunderstandings down the road. Complete proposals help you **nail down** details as well as land great jobs.

A good business proposal delivers a clear and compelling message about the abilities and services of your company. It does that in the following ways:

◇ It offers an "**unbiased**" observation of what the client needs. In the process, you may discover a solution they haven't considered before, adding value to your relationship with them.

◇ It clearly outlines a solution to the consumer's "challenge at hand", incorporating your business as an essential part of that solution.

◇ It backs up your proposed solution with a discussion of the capabilities of your business as well as market research related to the proposal.

◇ It shows that your experience puts you ahead of the competition in your ability to meet the client's goals.

In addition, the way you present your business in this proposal will shape the success or failure of all future relationships with target buyers. To earn their respect and attention, your proposal must show that you have a keen understanding of the prospective customer's needs.

Focus on the fact that your business is very well-equipped to handle their needs in the most effective and efficient manner possible. Make the time investment—conduct research to gain a full understanding of the nature and scope of the customer's requirements. Then present your ideas in a manner that **convinces** them that your product or service represents the best possible solution.

Most importantly, you have to differentiate your business from the competition. Some benefits to include are: the timeliness in which you plan to deliver your solutions and your documented experience and/or expertise in dealing with similar challenges (through case studies, third-party **endorsements**, and other supporting materials).

**单词注释**

nail down 确定
unbiased 公正的
convince 说服
endorsement 担保

While the work involved in creating a great proposal may seem **daunting** and time consuming, you have to consider the valuable pay-off for your business. The care you take in **tailoring** the proposal to prospect's unique needs is meant to serve as an **indication** of the level of service that they'll receive from you. And your prospects are bound to take notice of that extra effort.

单词注释

daunting 令人生畏的
tailor 专门制作，定做
indication 象征
glossary 词汇表

## 4. Key to Your Business Proposal 商务项目计划书的要领

Up to now you should have handed in all the 8 assignments to your tutor, which means you've done all the researches for the project, and you are ready to write the business proposal as the final task required.

However, your proposal would sum up the findings you have done in order to carry out the plan, covering what you are proposing to do, how you are planning to do it, when you will start, how long it will take, and how much you estimate it is going to cost. Thus, you may once again go through the information that you have collected, omit all the business opportunities and objectives that you cannot fulfill at present, and make certain you know exactly what you are going to do.

There is one key point for you to remember. That is: if your proposed project involves the use of technologies, be very careful with your explanation. The readers may have little or no technological background. Therefore, before you start to write the proposal, make sure you know who your readers will be and put your proposal in the language suitable to them. For example, if the proposal is technical and part of the readers are experts on the subject but part are not, you may write in technical or non-technical language, depending on who the immediate readers will be. In the former case, you should provide an executive summary in non-technical language and attach a **glossary** of the technical terms that have appeared in the proposal, or an appendix explaining the technical information, or both.

Your own business proposal should also consist of three parts: an introduction, a body, and a conclusion.

Remember, a key to write a good business proposal is to know why you are writing it in the first place. Identify what are the key things you need to communicate in order to persuade your reader. Your main objective behind writing a business proposal should be to express your ideas effectively. In the introduction, therefore, you should clearly present the problems that are to result in the project and the solution to them. You may also include the benefits that the project can bring about and the total estimated costs.

Then in the body, you should explain in detail how the project will be implemented, what methods and materials are going to be used, and when the project will start and end. You should present the cost breakdown for the entire job in this section. Such information can help the readers to think about the proposal and may stimulate them to approve it.

At last, you should emphasize the benefits that the project can create and urge the readers to approve it or take action. You should use a tone in your writing that tends to be encouraging, confident, **rational** and **assertive**.

单词注释

rational 合理的，理性的
assertive 果断的

## 5. Sample for Business Proposal 商务项目计划书示例

Below is a sample proposal for you to refer to. Pay attention to the way it organizes the ideas and develops the arguments.

# Proposal for
# Mini-Swallow Grocery Expansion

Prepared for

Mr. Victor Liu

Senior Vice President

West Area Branch Office

Industrial and Commercial Bank of China

Prepared by

Henry Zhang

Manager of

Mini-Swallow Grocery

Tel：0750–376××××

Fax：0750–379××××

E-mail：Henryz@gmail.com

Jan. 20th，20××

## Table of Contents

Mini-Swallow Grocery, established in 2005, is a privately owned business which lies on the campus of Jiangmen Polytechnic. It majors mainly in foodstuffs, various household supplies and office supplies for students, teachers, staff and local residents around. It is located between the police station and Student Dormitory 2 and right in the center of the campus by the West River. A great number of customers pay a visit to it every day.

In 2005, the store was granted the first loan of RMB350,000 for launching business. By the end of 2007, half of the loan had been paid back, nearly one year ahead of the schedule due to the increased enrollment during the past two years. By the end of 2009, the store had paid off the debt. From then on, the store has been running very well until 2014, when the revenue went down by 20%.

Through research, we find that the store only takes up an area of 80 square meters, in which only two thirds can be used as working area and one third as storage room, which has been greatly preventing the store from expanding its business and services. That's why many customers often complain about its narrow space, poor equipment, bad smell, lack of some daily supplies and shortage of services.

Therefore, to expand the store's operating area is believed to be the only solution. However, this expansion needs at least another loan of RMB300,000 to complete according to the budget. That's why the management asks again for the help of your bank. Due to the rapid growth of this college, we are sure to pay off the entire loan in two years after the project has finished as we have done for the first loan from your bank before.

## I. Introduction

The management plans to expand Mini-Swallow Grocery at Jiangmen Polytechnic, because we have found that the present site is really too small to meet the customers' needs, which greatly hinders the growth of our business.

The best solution to the problems is to expand the store, so that the management can hire 5 more employees to handle more stock and offer various services often demanded by customers in a larger place.

Thus we are planning to move the store to a new site that is about 350 square meters so that we will offer new services demanded by customers.

We are sure that this expanding project will bring us increases in revenue and profit by 50% and 60% respectively in the first year and will do more in the years to come.

However, the store needs a loan of about RMB 300, 000 to remodel the new store, purchase new equipment, stock with more variety of goods, hire more staff and offer new services.

The new store will surely satisfy the customers' needs, increase the revenue and profit, and improve the financial statements.

## Ⅱ. The Body

### Part 1 Findings and Analysis

### 1.1 Current Business Analysis

#### 1.1.1 The current state of the business

Mini-Swallow Grocery, established in 2005, is a privately owned business which lies on the campus of Jiangmen Polytechnic. It majors mainly in foodstuffs, various household supplies and office supplies for students, teachers, staff and local residents. It is located between the police station and Student Dormitory 2 and right in the center of the campus by the West River. A large number of customers would pay a visit to it every day.

However, the store only takes up an area of 80 square meters, in which only two thirds can be used as working area and one third as storage room, which has been greatly preventing the store from expanding its services. The management tried many times to offer a wider range of services, but failed each time because of the narrow space, which caused 20% of the revenue down in 2013, and thus makes us urgently feel it is high time to expand the store before it is too late.

### 1.1.2 Current business analysis

The major business of the store now is selling foodstuffs, various household supplies and office supplies for students, teachers and staff and local residents. In normal case, the store's warehouse can keep a stock of 50,000 pieces of goods, which is now getting farther and farther from enough due to the growing number of students and teachers and staff year by year.

There are only 10 workers in the store, including a manager, an accountant, 7 shop-assistants and a door keeper. They are always as busy as bees.

### 1.1.3 Financial performance

The financial performance has improved a good deal since the store opened. The revenue in 2008, at RMB 500,000, increased by 30% over the 2007 level of RMB 350,000.

Profits went up by 25%, while costs went down by 8%, thanks to the effective cost-cutting measures initiated at the beginning of 2008. The inventory turnover ratio has reached 7 times and the profit margin on sales 5%, well above the average of 5 times and 4% respectively.

As you know, the store was granted the first loan of RMB350,000 for launching business in 2005. By the end of 2007, half of the loan had been paid back, nearly one year ahead of the schedule due to the increased number of students and local people during the past two years. The store had paid off the debt by the end of 2009 based on the current cash flow.

### 1.1.4 Complaints and requests from customers

It is the lack of space that makes the store unable to increase its stock, and hire more employees to expand its services. That's why customers often express their dissatisfaction. Their main complaints are as follows:

◇The store is too small. They often have to stay in line, waiting for some time to be served. Let alone enjoy wandering around in a leisurely and quiet way.

◇It is too far away from the students' dormitories. Besides, it is noisy and smelly during meal times because the students' dining hall stands too close to it.

◇The air in the store gets very stuffy. They can hardly stay long in the store.

◇Sometimes they have to go out of campus to get things that could not be provided in the store, such as phone cards, books, magazines, computer hardware and software, etc.

◇The number of the shop-assistants is far from enough. Besides, they are not so professional and kind as they are expected.

◇Customers often inquire if the store could offer college-branded items such as T-shirts, calendars, postcards, envelops, letter-sheets, etc.

◇A photocopying service is wanted by many customers since there is no such kind of services around, which often makes them go out of the campus.

### 1.1.5 Customer profiles

The majority of the customers of the store are students, including the following kinds:

◇Undergraduates, who account for 80% of the student population.

◇Full-time graduate students, who are a small percentage of the enrollment. However, the number of graduate students is growing much faster than that of undergraduates, because more and more job vacancies are only open to candidates with a master's degree.

◇Part-time graduate students, who only come to school on weekends.

◇Trainees, who come to school to attend intensive training programs on some specific subjects.

◇Foreign students, who are either studying for a college degree or to improve their Chinese.

Non-student customers include:

◇Teachers, staff, and retirees of the college.

◇Residents living around the college.

◇Workers from the factories around.

◇Part-time employees in the college such as the peasants who work as cleaners and gardeners.

### 1.2 Focus Group Minutes

In order to get a clearer picture of the views and opinions of customers, 5 focus groups were organized. The focus groups were organized as the following figure shows:

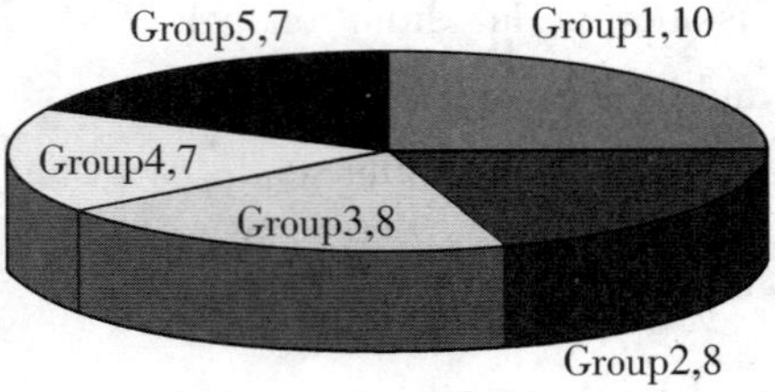


This figure shows we got:

Group 1: 10 undergraduate students;

Group 2: 8 graduate students;

Group 3: 8 college staff;

Group 4: 7 workers nearby;

Group 5: 7 local residents.

Since each of these categories of customers might have different expectations, views and needs, separate focus groups would be desirable. However, we believed that separate focus groups of men and women were of no use, for there would be no significant differences of opinions between them in a college environment.

Although a basic list of questions was prepared beforehand, the discussions with each focus group were allowed to be free and open.

Questions prepared are:

◇How many times do you visit the grocery store in a week?

◇How do you feel each time you pay a visit to the grocery store?

◇Do you usually find the goods you need?

◇What do you do when you can't find what you are looking for in the store?

◇What kinds of items are not offered now that you or your friends would like to buy?

◇What do you think of the prices the grocery store offers?

◇What kind of additional services would you like to see if the store could expand its services in the future?

◇What most often disappoints you when you come to the store?

◇What do you think of the business hours at present?

◇Do you think the shop assistants are helpful?

◇How do you expect the store to be remodeled when it reopens?

The responses to the questions above were positive and constructive for this expansion project.

Complaints gathered from the focus groups are:

◇The space of the store is so small that it is a suffering rather than an enjoyment to visit it.

◇The shop assistants, lacking work experience in a grocery store, often failed to give appropriate help when asked to do so.

◇Sometimes they have to go out of campus to get things that could not be provided in the store, such as phone cards, books, magazines, computer hardware and software, etc.

◇The present business hours are rather short. Students would prefer to visit the shop after the evening study sessions.

◇The number of the shop-assistants is far from enough. Besides, they are not so professional and kind as they are expected to be.

Suggestions gathered from the focus groups are:

◇The space of the store should be expanded at least half of the present size.

◇A photocopier and a printer as well as a public telephone

should be installed.

◇The aisles between the goods-shelves should be wider so as to let customers have enough walking space.

◇It's necessary to get the present store remodeled, which should be simple but comfortable.

◇Lighting and ventilation in the expanded store should be first-class.

◇The management should watch closely the latest products in order to have the latest and best products in stock.

◇The store should try to offer some college-branded items such as T-shirts, calendars, postcards, envelops, letter-sheets, envelops, etc.

### 1.3 Customer Surveys Design

| **Mini-Swallow Grocery** | | | | | |
|---|---|---|---|---|---|
| **Customer Survey**<br>Mini-Swallow Grocery is committed to customers' satisfaction and would like to know how well we're doing. Your answers will help us to identify areas needing improvement. If you have questions about this survey, please contact Henry Zhang (0750–3725208). Thank you for your time and comments. | | | | | |
| What is your overall satisfaction with Mini-Swallow Grocery? | | | | | |
| | 5 (Very satisfied) | 4 | 3 | 2 | 1 (Very dissatisfied) |
| | □ | □ | □ | □ | □ |
| How satisfied are you with the following areas? | | | | | |
| | 5 (Very satisfied) | 4 | 3 | 2 | 1 (Very dissatisfied) |
| The space | □ | □ | □ | □ | □ |
| The price | □ | □ | □ | □ | □ |
| Quality | □ | □ | □ | □ | □ |
| Business hours | □ | □ | □ | □ | □ |
| Ability to meet customers' needs | □ | □ | □ | □ | □ |

(continued)

| How satisfied are you with the environment of Mini-Swallow Grocery? | | | | | |
|---|---|---|---|---|---|
| | 5 (Very satisfied) | 4 | 3 | 2 | 1 (Very dissatisfied) |
| The lighting | ☐ | ☐ | ☐ | ☐ | ☐ |
| The color of the wall | ☐ | ☐ | ☐ | ☐ | ☐ |
| The ventilation | ☐ | ☐ | ☐ | ☐ | ☐ |
| The inner decoration | ☐ | ☐ | ☐ | ☐ | ☐ |
| The outer look | ☐ | ☐ | ☐ | ☐ | ☐ |

| Compared with the alternative services, our services are: | |
|---|---|
| ☐ | Much better. |
| ☐ | Somewhat better. |
| ☐ | About the same. |
| ☐ | Somewhat worse. |
| ☐ | Much worse. |
| **What do you think of the staff?** | |
| ☐ | Kind enough. |
| ☐ | Not so kind. |
| ☐ | Very experienced. |
| ☐ | Need to be trained. |
| **How often do you visit Mini-Swallow Grocery?** | |
| ☐ | Daily. |
| ☐ | Once a week or more. |
| ☐ | Two or three times per month. |
| ☐ | Several times a year. |
| ☐ | Once a year. |
| ☐ | Other: ________ |
| **What do you suggest us to do urgently to improve our service?** | |
| ☐ | Expand the store. |
| ☐ | Hire more skilled shop assistants. |
| ☐ | Remodel the store. |
| ☐ | Get more items to sell. |
| ☐ | Add after-sales services. |

(continued)

| Do you agree or disagree with the following statements? | |
|---|---|
| ☐ | The window displays are appealing. |
| ☐ | The store is well laid out. |
| ☐ | The signage is clear. |
| ☐ | The signage is informative. |
| ☐ | The store is clean and tidy. |
| ☐ | The store has a pleasant shopping atmosphere. |
| ☐ | The store is easy to move about in. |
| ☐ | There are sufficient checkouts. |

### 1.4 SWOT Analysis

Strengths:

◇The management of Mini-Swallow Grocery is given the exclusive right to run an on-campus groceries store.

◇The store serves the students and teachers who need stationery for their study and work every year.

◇The store has extensive contact with the students, teachers, staff and residents nearby, who would like to provide information on the goods needed at any time.

◇The store purchases directly from manufacturers, so it can offer larger discounts to the customers.

◇The rent of the store is not so high. This allows the store to lower prices.

Weaknesses:

◇The narrow space constrains the store from increasing stock and from offering more services.

◇Customers often do not have much choice when choosing items they want urgently.

◇It is impossible to expand the store at the present location, because the rooms around are all being occupied by the cafeteria that refuses to give any up.

◇The college did not have a plan to build a grocery store in the original place. Therefore, it is difficult to find an ideal site for the new store. It may end up in some building far from the center of the campus.

◇The manager, who used to work in a hotel, lacks experience of running a grocery.

Opportunities:

◇There are eight schools in this area, but there is no decent grocery store around.

◇There are more than ten thousand students and six hundred teachers and staff living in the campus. So we are sure to have enough customer resources.

◇The number of students at the college is growing rapidly due to the fact that the Chinese government is encouraging universities to enlarge their enrollment to satisfy the people's demand for higher education.

◇There are a great number of local residents and workers from many a factory nearby.

◇China has already joined the WTO and need qualified personnel to deal with the relevant issues as China becomes more integrated into the world community. The university has excellent programs to train such candidates.

◇It is difficult to find a place to make photocopies or print a document from a computer disk, especially in the evenings.

Threats:

◇A competitor is planning to open a supermarket just around the corner outside the college.

◇The shop assistants are not so experienced and kind, which often makes customers feel unsatisfied.

◇Goods prices are getting higher and higher recently, and it is getting more and more difficult to offer discounts to our customers.

◇Online shops that offer discount goods are attracting more and more customers.

## Part 2 Planning the Activities

### 2.1 The Action Plan

The project will start immediately after it is approved and the budget is available. It will take about eight weeks to implement the project. Here is the action plan table for reference:

| Task | Description | Order/Logic | Time |
|---|---|---|---|
| A | Identify and negotiate the rental of the new premises.<br>Sign the contract with the college. | To be completed first. | Week 1 |
| B | Design the new store layout.<br>Prepare for remodeling of the new store. | Start when A is completed. | Week 2 |
| C | Start remodeling the store.<br>Order new shelves, equipment and furniture and new goods. | Start when B is completed. | Week 3 |
| D | Hire the new shop assistants.<br>Start training the new shop assistants. | Start when C is completed. | W eek4 |
| E | Check and accept the remodeling project.<br>Publicize on campus store expansion. | Start when D is completed. | Week 5 |
| F | Get new equipment delivered and installed.<br>Clean the new store and pack up stock in the old store. | Start when E is completed. | Week 6 |
| G | Close the present store and move everything to the new store.<br>Put the old stock on the shelves.<br>Get the new stock delivered and put on the shelves. | Start when F is completed. | Week 7 |
| H | Hold the opening ceremony. | Start when G is completed. | Week 8 |

## 2.2 The Activity Flow Chart

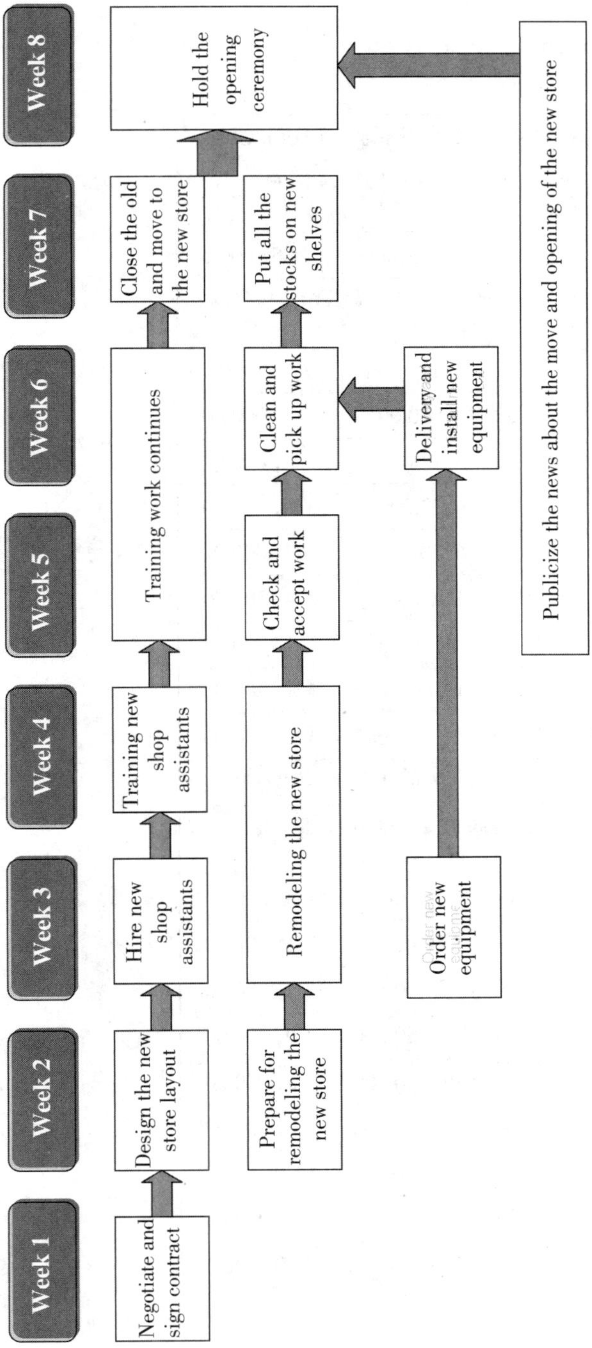

## 2. 3 Cost Breakdown

Listed below is the cost breakdown for the Mini-Swallow Grocery expansion project as requested:

| Item | Description | Quantity | Unit | Unit Price | Total Cost |
|---|---|---|---|---|---|
| Rental cost | The new premises would cost no less than RMB55, 000.00 to rent per year as shown in the following: | | | | |
| | Rental cost | | | Lump sum | ¥ 55, 000.00 |
| Remodeling | The remodeling costs for the new store would be RMB127,700 as shown in the following: | | | | |
| 1 | Labor cost | | | Lump sum | ¥ 75, 000.00 |
| 2 | Windows | 10 | set | ¥ 800.00 | ¥ 8, 000.00 |
| 3 | Flooring | 8,000 | $m^2$ | ¥ 1.00 | ¥ 8, 000.00 |
| 4 | Paint | 500 | kg | ¥ 12.00 | ¥ 6, 000.00 |
| 5 | Ceiling | 700 | $m^2$ | ¥ 10.00 | ¥ 7, 000.00 |
| 6 | Lumber | | | Lump sum | ¥ 4, 500.00 |
| 7 | Lighting | | | Lump sum | ¥ 15, 000.00 |
| 8 | Glue & tools | | | Lump sum | ¥ 1, 200.00 |
| 9 | Cement & putty | 6 | ton | Lump sum | ¥ 3, 000.00 |
| | | | | Sub-total: | ¥ 127, 700.00 |
| Equipment | The cost of equipment in the new bookshop would be RMB70, 300 as shown in the following: | | | | |
| 1 | Photocopier | 1 | set | ¥ 35, 000.00 | ¥ 35, 000.00 |
| 2 | Shelves | 500 | set | ¥ 30.00 | ¥ 15, 000.00 |
| 3 | Office furniture | 1 | set | ¥ 3, 000.00 | ¥ 3, 000.00 |
| 4 | Computers | 2 | set | ¥ 4, 500.00 | ¥ 9, 000.00 |
| 5 | Printers | 2 | set | ¥ 1, 500.00 | ¥ 3, 000.00 |
| 6 | Airconditioners | 2 | set | ¥ 2, 000.00 | ¥ 4, 0000.00 |
| 7 | Armchairs | 3 | set | ¥ 100.00 | ¥ 300.00 |
| 8 | Office supplies | 1 | set | ¥ 1, 000.00 | ¥ 1, 000.00 |
| | | | | Sub-total: | ¥ 70, 300.00 |

(continued)

| Budget | The annual increase in the operating budget would be RMB35, 300 as shown in the following: | | | | |
|---|---|---|---|---|---|
| 1 | Wages | | | Lump sum | ¥ 28, 000.00 |
| 2 | Utilities | | | Lump sum | ¥ 3, 000.00 |
| 3 | Equipment maintenance | | | Lump sum | ¥ 1, 500.00 |
| 4 | Consultant fees | | | Lump sum | ¥ 2, 800.00 |
| | | | | Sub-total: | ¥ 35, 300.00 |
| Total cost of the whole project = Initial costs + Recurrent costs = RMB288, 300 as shown in the following: | | | | | |
| Intial costs | Remodeling | | | Lump sum | ¥ 127, 700.00 |
| | Equipment | | | Lump sum | ¥ 70, 300.00 |
| | | | | Sub-total: | ¥ 198, 000.00 |
| Recurrent costs | Rental | | | Lump sum | ¥ 55, 000.00 |
| | Operating budget | | | Lump sum | ¥ 35, 300.00 |
| | | | | Sub-total: | ¥ 90, 300.00 |
| | | | | Total: | ¥ 288, 300.00 |

## 2. 4 Risk Analysis & Management

Before putting the plan into practice, the management finds that the following problems might affect the successful completion of the project. These problems, also called risks, generally fall into three categories:

**(1) People-related.**

◇The new employees may not be good at selling at all.

◇Some dishonest students may pilfer from the store.

◇The clerks next door may not be so happy with the noises resulting from the remodeling of the new site and may demand no remodeling during the working hours.

**(2) Time-related.**

◇The university may shorten the period of the lease of the new site and even worse, expropriate the new store.

◇The loan may not be obtained from the bank in time, so the

workers may not be paid on time, which may cause the delay of this project.

◇The newly ordered shelves may not arrive in time, causing delay in the opening of the new store.

◇The weather may turn to be bad, which may slow down the seed of remodeling.

(3) **Product-related.**

◇The supply channels may be blocked, which may result in the rise of prices.

◇The paint applied to the walls may not live up to the quality and begin to fall off shortly after the decoration.

◇The new stock may not cater to the interests of the customer.

Since it's impossible to eradicate all these risks, the store manager has to control and manage them. Here are three measures to be taken.

◇Carry out a market research. In order to prevent the dangers from happening, we'll carry out a market research among our target customers so that we can improve the popularity of the stock and remain constant contact with the instructors to get the latest information of products and the market.

◇Be ready to deal with the urgency. Prepare alternatives beforehand in case the dangers actually happen. We will keep contacting more clerk candidates as substitutes in case the employed are not qualified. What's more, try our best to finish the remodeling within the weekends before the dissatisfaction occurred from the neighboring clerks.

◇Set aside a certain percentage of the total budget as contingency allowance to take account of the unexpected risks, such as to cover the pilferage loss and to cover the repainting expense.

After the risk analysis, we think three more items should be added to the total costs:

| | |
|---|---|
| Public relations | 3,000 yuan per annum |
| Market research | 2,000 yuan per annum |
| Contingency allowance | 1% of the annual profit |

So the total cost of the project would be:

RMB288, 300 +5, 000+1% of the annual profit.

That is about RMB300, 000.

## Ⅲ. Conclusion

Our careful investigation indicates that the expansion project will greatly increase the turnover and profit, as well as improve our financial statements. Therefore, we are able to pay off the entire debt within the deadline as we have done for the first loan.

Finally, I would like to make an appointment with you at any time this month to discuss the details of this plan and will be quite happy to provide any additional information that you may be interested in. Please tell me the most convenient time for me to call on you. I will always be ready to discuss with you on this expansion project. It is highly appreciated to hear from you soon.

## Ⅳ. Bibliography

[1] John Hilton，羡锡彪. 实用商务项目设计. 北京：中央广播电视大学出版社，2001.

[2] Mary Ellen Guffey. 国际商务交际. 北京：中央广播电视大学出版社，2004.

[3] http：//www.bizhelp24.com.

[4] http：//www.ider.herts.ac.uk.

[5] http：//www.statistics.gov.

## Ⅴ. Acknowledgement

(omitted)

## Ⅵ. Appendix

Assignment 1 (omitted)

Assignment 2 （omitted）
Assignment 3 （omitted）
Assignment 4 （omitted）
Assignment 5 （omitted）
Assignment 6 （omitted）
Assignment 7 （omitted）
Assignment 8 （omitted）

## The List of the 8 Assignments to Be Handed within the Deadline

①Analysis of the business (financial situation, current stock movement, real estimates of the finances of the business and the customer profile) (10%)

②Focus groups minute (10%)

③Customer surveys design (5%)

④SWOT analysis (10%)

⑤Action plan (5%)

⑥Activity flow chart (5%)

⑦Cost breakdown (5%)

⑧Risk analysis (10%)

---

Total marks: 60 %

Hand in your final proposal to your tutor without fail! (40%)

## Appendix One

Student's Practice 1[①]
(扩建项目实例)

# Proposal for Chen-pi Store Expansion

Prepared for Victor
General Manager
China Construction Bank

Prepared by Susan
Manager
East Lake Department Store

Tel：0750-372××××
Fax：0750-370××××
E-mail：joanchen@126.com
Date：May 5th, 2008

① "Student's Practice" 学生实践篇的资料均为原始资料，指导老师尚未作详细批改，所以会出现许多语法、词汇等方面的错误，特此说明。

## Table of Contents

**Abstract**

Chen-pi store, established in 2007, is a privately owned business which lies on the Palace International of Jiangmen Polytechnic. It majors in cake, sauce, tea, wine which are made with Chen-pi. It is located in No.18 – 28, Donghua Second Road, Jiangmen city, Guangdong province, the opposite of the East Park, and a large number of customers pay a visit it every day.

Chen-pi series is for health natural character. It made the orthodox school Xinhui dried mandarin peel, and has the healthy care effect. The formula of Chen-pi is uniquely, and the taste of it is not greasy but fragrant, sweet and mellow.

It is firmly believed that this expansion plan would enable us not only to meet the demands and needs of the customers on and around the campus but also of those in other areas. There is only one Chen-pi store in Jiang-men. A well-equipped store like this one would attract customers from local residential areas and other areas. With the new store's capacity, we would still have room to expand when new business opportunities appear.

**I. Introduction**

Chen-pi store plans to move the store to Jiangmen Palace International, because we have found that the present site is really too small to meet customers' needs, which greatly hinders our business growth.

The best solution to the problems is to expand the Chen-pi store, so that the management can hire 6 more employees to handle more stock and offer various services often demanded by customers in a larger place.

Thus we are planning to move the store to a new site that is about 300 square meters so that we will offer new services demanded by customers.

We are sure this expanding project will bring us increases in revenue and profit by 50% and 60% respectively in the first year and will do more in the years to come.

However, the store needs a loan of RMB300, 000 to remodel the new store, purchase new equipment, stock with a more variety of goods and offer new services.

The new store will surely satisfy the customers' needs, increase the revenue and profit, and improve the financial statements.

**II. The Body**

## Part 1 Findings and Analysis

### 1.1 Current Business Analysis

#### 1.1.1 The current state of the business

Chen-pi store, established in 2007, is a privately owned business which lies on the Palace International of Jiangmen Polytechnic. It majors in cake, sauce, tea, wine which are mixed with Chen-pi. It is located in No.18 – 28, Donghua Second Road, Jiangmen city, Guangdong province, opposite of the East Park, and a large number of customers pay a visit to it every day.

Chen-pi series is for health natural character. It makes the orthodox school Xinhui dried mandarin peel, and has the healthy care effect. The formula of Chen-pi is unique, and the taste of it is not only greasy but also fragrant, sweet and mellow.

However, the store only takes up an area of 30 square meters, in which there are only one long counter and one long closet, and the warehouse is separate from the store. Besides it is not big enough to show the goods.

#### 1.1.2 Current business analysis

The major business of the store now is selling various series of Chen-pi products, for example, Chen-pi cake, Chen-pi pastry, Chen-pi green tea cake, Chen-pi Mandarin orange jam, Chen-pi sauce, Chen-pi Pu Erh tea and Xinhui mandarin peel win. In normal case, the store's warehouse can keep a stock of 50, 000 pieces of goods, which is now getting much farther from enough due to the growing number of customers year by year.

The financial performance has improved a good deal since the

Chen-pi store opened. The revenue was increased year by year. In 2007, the Chen-pi store was granted a loan of 350, 000 yuan for launching the business. By the end of 2008, the loan had been paid back. The store has paid off the debt by the end of 2009 based on the current cash flow.

There are only 6 workers in the Chen-pi store, including one manager, one accountant, 3 shop-assistants and one deliveryman. They are always very busy.

### 1.1.3 Customer profiles

The majorities of customers buy these Chen-pi special local products due to present a gift to clients, friends, boss and so on.

◇Natives: buy these special local products for friends who are out comer.

◇Outcomers: buy for family when come back home.

◇Many people hold meetings in the Palace International, and after meeting they buy some Chen-pi special local products to clients.

◇Frequent visitors: somebody loves to eat the Chen-pi special local products and always visit our store.

### 1.1.4 Complaints and requests from customers

There is only one Chen-pi store in Jiangmen, because these Chen-pi special local products have applied patented product, and many people complain that:

◇The store is too small. They often have to stay in line, waiting for some time to be served.

◇It is too far away from to the center of city.

◇The customers often inquire if the Chen-pi store could offer other items such as cigarette, map, etc.

## 1.2 Focus Group Minutes

In order to get a clearer picture of the views and opinions of customers, five focus groups were organized. The focus groups were as follows:

Group 1: 10 natives

Group 2: 8 out comers

Group 3: 8 frequent visitors

Group 4: 7 clients

Group 5: 7 hotel staff

Since each of these categories of customers might have different expectations, views and needs, separate focus groups would be desirable.

Anyhow, a basic list of questions was prepared beforehand, but the discussions with each focus group were allowed to be free and open.

Questions prepared are:

◇How many times do you visit the Chen-pi store every week?

◇How do you feel each time you pay a visit to the Chen-pi store?

◇What do you think of the Chen-pi special local products?

◇What kinds of items are not offered now that you or your friends would like to buy?

◇What do you think of the prices the Chen-pi store offers?

◇What kind of additional services would you like to see if the Chen-pi store could expand its services in the future?

◇What most often disappoints you when you come to the Chen-pi store?

◇What do you think of the business hours at present?

◇Do you think the shop assistants are helpful?

The responses to the questions above were positive and constructive for this expansion project.

Complaints gathered from the focus groups is:

◇There are two people work in the Chen-pi store everyday, and sometimes the shop assistants are too busy to serve the customers waiting.

## 1.3 Customer Surveys Design

| Chen-pi Store | | | | | |
|---|---|---|---|---|---|
| **Customer Survey**<br>Chen-pi store is committed to customer satisfaction and would like to know how well we're doing. Your answers will help us to identify areas needing improvement. If you have questions about this survey, please contact Susan (0750 – 3725208). Thank you for your time and comments. | | | | | |
| What is your overall satisfaction with Chen-pi store? | | | | | |
| | 5 (Very satisfied) | 4 | 3 | 2 | 1 (Very dissatisfied) |
| | □ | □ | □ | □ | □ |
| How satisfied are you with the following areas? | | | | | |
| | 5 (Very satisfied) | 4 | 3 | 2 | 1 (Very dissatisfied) |
| The space | □ | □ | □ | □ | □ |
| The price | □ | □ | □ | □ | □ |
| Quality | □ | □ | □ | □ | □ |
| Business hours | □ | □ | □ | □ | □ |
| Ability to meet customers' needs | □ | □ | □ | □ | □ |
| How satisfied are you with the environment of Chen-pi store? | | | | | |
| | 5 (Very satisfied) | 4 | 3 | 2 | 1 (Very dissatisfied) |
| The lighting | □ | □ | □ | □ | □ |
| The color of the chest | □ | □ | □ | □ | □ |
| The ventilation | □ | □ | □ | □ | □ |
| The inner decoration | □ | □ | □ | □ | □ |
| The outer look | □ | □ | □ | □ | □ |
| Compared to the alternative services, our services are: | | | | | |
| □ | much better. | | | | |
| □ | somewhat better. | | | | |
| □ | about the same. | | | | |

(continued)

| | |
|---|---|
| ☐ | somewhat worse. |
| ☐ | much worse. |
| What do you think of the staff? | |
| ☐ | Kind enough. |
| ☐ | Not so kind. |
| ☐ | Very experienced. |
| ☐ | Need to be trained. |
| How often do you visit Chen-pi store? | |
| ☐ | Daily. |
| ☐ | Once a week or more. |
| ☐ | Two or three times per month. |
| ☐ | Several times a year. |
| ☐ | Once a year. |
| ☐ | Other: ____________ |
| What do you suggest us to do urgently to improve our service? | |
| ☐ | Expand the store. |
| ☐ | Hire more skilled shop assistants. |
| ☐ | Remodel the store. |
| ☐ | Get more items to sell. |
| ☐ | Add after sales services. |
| Do you agree or disagree with the following statements? | |
| ☐ | The window displays are appealing. |
| ☐ | The store is well laid out. |
| ☐ | The signage is clear. |
| ☐ | The signage is informative. |
| ☐ | The store is clean and tidy. |
| ☐ | The store has a pleasant shopping atmosphere. |
| ☐ | The store is easy to move about in. |
| ☐ | There are sufficient checkouts. |

## 1.4 SWOT Analysis

Strengths:

◇The management of Chen-pi store is given the exclusive right to run a Chen-pi special local product store.

◇The store serves the customers who need buy some Jiangmen special local products.

◇The store has extensive contact with the customers, who provide information on the goods needed.

◇The store purchases directly from manufacturers, so it can offer larger discounts to the customers.

◇The rent of the store is free, because the store belongs to the Palace International.

Weaknesses:

◇The narrow space constrains the store from increasing stock and from offering more services.

◇It is impossible to expand the store at the present location, because the space program of the hotel lobby hasn't been changed right now.

Opportunities:

◇There is only one Chen-pi store which has various kinds of special local products in Jiangmen.

◇There is a large of passenger flow every day in the Palace International.

◇The number of visitors is growing rapidly due to the fact that people have more and more holidays.

◇More and more tour groups visit the Palace International.

◇There are great number of companies nearby.

◇China has already joined the WTO and needs qualified personnel to deal with the relevant issues as China becomes more integrated into the world community. The hotel has excellent programs to train such candidates.

◇It is difficult to find a place to buy such kinds of Chen-pi special local products in Jiangmen.

Threats:

◇Many competitors are planning to open such Jiangmen special local product in Jiangmen.

◇The shop assistants are not so experienced, because the hotel always changes the employees.

◇Goods prices are getting higher and higher recently. So it is getting more and more difficult to offer discounts to our customers.

◇Online shops that offer discount goods are attracting more and more customers.

**Part 2 Planning the Activities**

**2.1 The Action Plan**

It will take 8 weeks to implement the project after it is approved.

| Task | Description | Order/Logic | Time |
|---|---|---|---|
| A | Sign the contract with the hotel. | To be completed first. | Week 1 |
| B | Design the new store layout.<br>Prepare for the remodeling of the new store. | Start when A is completed. | Week 2 |
| C | Start remodeling the store.<br>Order new shelves, equipment and furniture and new goods.<br>Hire the new shop assistants. | Start when B is completed. | Week 3 |
| D | Start training the new shop assistants. | Start when C is completed. | Week 4 |
| E | Check and accept the remodeling project.<br>Publicize on campus store expansion. | Start when D is completed. | Week 5 |
| F | Get the new equipment delivered and installed.<br>Clean the new store and pack up stock in the old store. | Start when E is completed. | Week 6 |

(continued)

| Task | Description | Order/Logic | Time |
|---|---|---|---|
| G | Close the present store and move everything to the new store. Put the old stock on the shelves. Get the new stock delivered and put on the selves. | Start when F is completed. | Week 7 |
| H | Hold the opening ceremony. | Start when G is completed. | Week 8 |

## 2. 2  The Activity Flow Chart

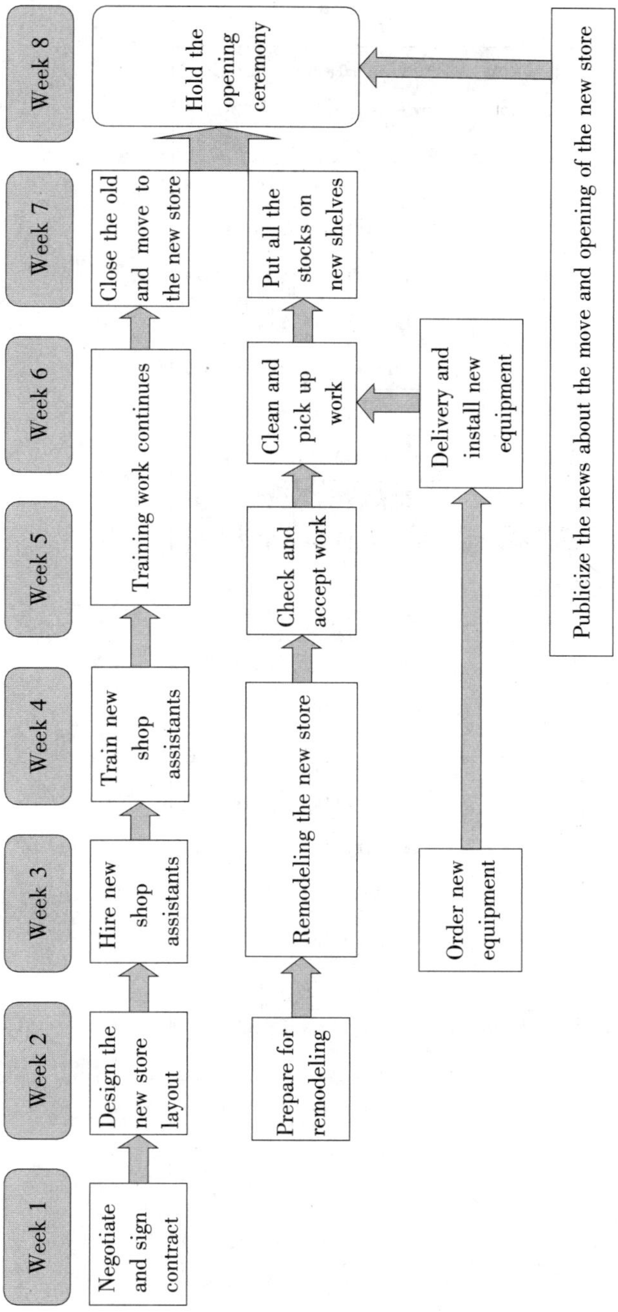

## 2. 3 Cost Breakdown

| Item | Description | Quantity | Unit | Unit Price | Total Cost |
|---|---|---|---|---|---|
| Remodeling | The remodeling costs for the new store would be RMB67, 500 as shown in the following: | | | | |
| 1 | Labor cost | | | Lump sum | ¥48, 000.00 |
| 2 | Flooring | 100 | $m^2$ | ¥50.00 | ¥5, 000.00 |
| 3 | Paint | 200 | kg | ¥10.00 | ¥2, 000.00 |
| 5 | Lumber | | | Lump sum | ¥1, 500.00 |
| 6 | Lighting | | | Lump sum | ¥8, 000.00 |
| 7 | Glue & tools | | | Lump sum | ¥2, 000.00 |
| 8 | Cement & putty | 5 | ton | ¥200.00 | ¥1, 000.00 |
| | | | | Sub-total: | ¥67, 500.00 |
| Equipment | The cost of equipment in the new bookshop would be RMB38, 800 as shown in the following: | | | | |
| 1 | Photocopier | 1 | ea | ¥3, 500.00 | ¥3, 500.00 |
| 2 | Shelves | 500 | ea | ¥30.00 | ¥15, 000.00 |
| 3 | Office furniture | 1 | set` | ¥3, 000.00 | ¥3, 000.00 |
| 4 | Computers | 2 | ea | ¥4, 500.00 | ¥9, 000.00 |
| 5 | Printers | 2 | ea | ¥1, 500.00 | ¥3, 000.00 |
| 6 | Air conditioners | 2 | ea | ¥2, 000.00 | ¥4, 000.00 |
| 7 | Armchairs | 3 | ea | ¥100.00 | ¥300.00 |
| 8 | Office supplies | 1 | set | ¥1, 000.00 | ¥1, 000.00 |
| | | | | Sub-total: | ¥38, 800.00 |
| Budget | The annual increase in the operating budget would be RMB35, 300 as shown in the following: | | | | |
| 1 | Wages | | | Lump sum | ¥28, 000.00 |
| 2 | Utilities | | | Lump sum | ¥3, 000.00 |
| 3 | Equipment maintenance | | | Lump sum | ¥1, 500.00 |
| 4 | Consultant fees | | | Lump sum | ¥2, 800.00 |
| | | | | Sub-total: | ¥35, 300.00 |

(continued)

| | | | | | |
|---|---|---|---|---|---|
| Total cost of the whole project = Initial costs + Recurrent costs = RMB106, 300 as shown in the following: | | | | | |
| Initial costs | Remodeling | | | Lump sum | ¥67, 500.00 |
| | Equipment | | | Lump sum | ¥38, 800.00 |
| | | | | Sub-total: | ¥106, 300.00 |
| Recurrent costs: | Rental | | Mon. | Lump sum | ¥50, 00.00 |
| | Operating budget | | | Lump sum | ¥35, 000.00 |
| | | | | Sub-total: | ¥85, 000.00 |
| | | | | Total: | ¥191, 300.00 |

### 2.4 Risk Analysis & Management

Before putting the plan into practice, the manager finds that the following problems might affect the successful completion of the project. These problems, also called risks, generally fall into three categories:

(1) **People-related.**

◇The new employees may not be good at selling goods at all.

◇Some customers may pilfer from the Chen-pi store.

◇The clerks next door may not be happy with the noises resulting from the remodeling of the new site and may demand no remodeling during the working hours.

(2) **Time-related.**

◇The university may shorten the period of the lease of the new site and even worse, expropriate the new store.

(3) **Product-related.**

◇The loan may not be obtained from the bank in time.

◇The paint applied to the walls may not live up to the quality and begin to fall off shortly after the decoration.

◇The new stock may not cater to the interests of the customer.

Since it's impossible to eradicate all these risks, the store manager thinks he has to control and manage them. Now, he has figured out three measures:

◇Try to avoid the risks, i. e. to prevent the threats from

happening, say, carrying out market research among target customers to improve the popularity of the stock and remaining constant contact with the instructors to get the latest information.

◇Prepare alternatives beforehand in case the dangers actually happen, say, contacting more clerk candidates as substitutes in case the employed are not qualified and trying to finish the remodeling within the weekends if the dissatisfaction occurred from the neighboring clerks.

◇Set aside a certain percentage of the total budget as contingency allowance to take account of the unexpected risks, such as to cover the pilferage loss and to cover the repainting expense.

After the risk analysis, we think three more items should be added to the total costs:

| | |
|---|---|
| Public relations | 2, 000 yuan per annum |
| Market research | 1, 000 yuan per annum |
| Contingency allowance | 1% of the annual profit |

So that would be: RMB315, 600.00+3, 000+1% of the annual profit.

## Ⅲ. Conclusion

In conclusion, it is firmly believed that this expansion plan would enable us not only to meet the demands and needs of the customers in Jiangmen but also of those in this area. There is only one Chen-pi store in Jiangmen. A well-equipped store like this would attract customers from local residential areas and other areas. With the new store's capacity, we would still have room to expand when new business opportunities appear.

The project will bring increases in revenue by around 35% in the first year and will be even more successful in the years to come.

The new business place needs an investment of RMB350, 000

or so in the first year to rent the premises, make decoration, hire more experienced employees and train the staff, purchase the new equipment and furniture, stock a great deal of new products and offer more services as well.

Our careful investigation indicates that the expansion project will meet the customers' needs, greatly increase the turnover and profit, as well as improve the financial statements.

Finally, I would like to make an appointment with you at any time this month to discuss the details of this plan and will be quite happy to provide any additional information that you may be interested in. Please tell me the most convenient time for me to call on you. I will always be ready to discuss with you on this expansion project. It is highly appreciated to hear from you soon.

## Ⅳ. Bibliography

[1] John Hilton，羡锡彪. 实用商务项目设计. 北京：中央广播电视大学出版社，2001.

[2] Mary Ellen Guffey. 国际商务交际. 北京：中央广播电视大学出版社，2004.

[3] http：//www.bizhelp24.com

[4] http：//www.ider.herts.ac.uk

[5] http：//www.statistics.gov.

## Ⅴ. Acknowledgement

(omitted)

## Ⅵ. Appendix

### Assignment 1 The current state of the business

Chen-pi store, established in 2007, is a privately owned business which lies on the Palace International of Jiangmen Polytechnic. It majors mainly in cake, sauce, tea, wine which is made with Chen-pi. It is located in No.18 – 28, Donghua Second Road, Jiangmen city, Guangdong province, the opposite of the East

Park, and a large number of customers pay a visit it every day.

Chen-pi series is for health natural character. It made the orthodox school Xinhui dried mandarin peel, and has the healthy care effect. The formula of Chen-pi is uniquely, and the taste of it is not greasy but fragrant, sweet and mellow.

However, the store only takes up an area of 30 square meters, which includes only one long vitrine and one long closet, and the warehouse is separate from it, but it is enough to show the goods.

**1. Current Business Analysis**

The major business of the store now is selling various series of Chen-pi products, for example, Chen-pi cake, Chen-pi pastry, Chen-pi green tea cake, Chen-pi mandarin orange jam, Chen-pi sauce, Chen-pi Pu Erh Tea and Xinhui mandarin peel win. In normal case, the store's warehouse can keep a stock of 50, 000 pieces of goods, which is now getting much farther from enough due to the growing number of customers year by year.

The financial performance has improved a good deal since the Chen-pi store opened. The revenue was increased year by year. In 2007, the Chen-pi store was granted a loan of 350, 000 yuan for launching the business. By the end of 2008, the loan had been paid back; the store will have paid off the debt by the end of 2009 based on the current cash flow.

There are only 6 workers in the Chen-pi store, including one manager, one accountant, 3 shop-assistants and one deliveryman. They are always kept very busy.

**2. Customer Profiles**

The majorities of the customers buy these Chen-pi special local products due to present a gift to clients, friends or boss and so on.

◇Natives: buy these special local products for friends who are out comers.

◇Outcomers: buy for family when come back home.

◇Many people hold the meeting in the Palace International, and after meeting they buy some Chen-pi special local products to clients.

◇Frequent visitors: somebody loves to eat the Chen-pi special local products and always visit our store.

Complaints and Requests from Customers:

There is only one Chen-pi store in Jiangmen, because these Chen-pi special local products had applied patented product, and many people complaint that:

◇The store is too small. They often have to stay in line, waiting for some time to be served.

◇It is too far away from to the center of city.

◇The customers often inquire if the Chen-pi store could offer other items such as cigarette, map, etc.

**Assignment 2 Focus group minutes**

In order to get a clearer picture of the views and opinions of customers, five focus groups were organized. The focus groups were as follows:

Group 1: 10 natives

Group 2: 8 outcomers

Group 3: 8 frequent visitors

Group 4: 7 clients

Group 5: 7 hotel staff

Since each of these categories of customer might have different expectations, views and needs, separate focus groups would be desirable.

Anyhow, a basic list of questions was prepared beforehand, but the discussions with each focus group were allowed to be free and open.

Questions prepared are:

◇How many times do you visit the Chen-pi store in a week?

◇How do you feel each time you pay a visit to the Chen-pi store?

◇How do you think about the Chen-pi special local product?

◇What kinds of items are not offered now, and which kinds you or your friends would like to buy?

◇What do you think of the prices the grocery store offers?

◇What kind of additional services would you like to see if the

Chen-pi store could expand its services in the future?

◇What most often disappoints you when you come to the Chen-pi store?

◇What do you think of the business hours at present?

◇Do you think the shop assistants are helpful?

The responses to the questions above were positive and constructive for this expansion project.

Complaint gathered from the focus groups is:

◇There are two people work in the Chen-pi store everyday, and sometimes the shop assistants are too busy to serve the customers.

### Assignment 3 Customer surveys design

| **Chen-pi Store** | | | | | |
|---|---|---|---|---|---|
| **Customer Survey**<br>Chen-pi store is committed to customer satisfaction and would like to know how well we're doing. Your answers will help us to identify areas needing improvement. If you have questions about this survey, please contact Henry Zhang (0750-3725208). Thank you for your time and comments. | | | | | |
| What is your overall satisfaction with Chen-pi store? | | | | | |
| | 5<br>Very satisfied | 4 | 3 | 2 | 1<br>Very dissatisfied |
| | □ | □ | □ | □ | □ |
| How satisfied are you with the following areas? | | | | | |
| | 5<br>Very satisfied | 4 | 3 | 2 | 1<br>Very dissatisfied |
| The space | □ | □ | □ | □ | □ |
| The price | □ | □ | □ | □ | □ |
| Quality | □ | □ | □ | □ | □ |
| Business hours | □ | □ | □ | □ | □ |
| Ability to meet customers' needs | □ | □ | □ | □ | □ |

(continued)

| How satisfied are you with the environment of Chen-pi store? | | | | | |
|---|---|---|---|---|---|
| | 5<br>Very satisfied | 4 | 3 | 2 | 1<br>Very dissatisfied |
| The lighting | ☐ | ☐ | ☐ | ☐ | ☐ |
| The color of the chest | ☐ | ☐ | ☐ | ☐ | ☐ |
| The ventilation | ☐ | ☐ | ☐ | ☐ | ☐ |
| The inner decoration | ☐ | ☐ | ☐ | ☐ | ☐ |
| The outer look | ☐ | ☐ | ☐ | ☐ | ☐ |

| Compared to the alternative services, our services are: | |
|---|---|
| ☐ | Much better. |
| ☐ | Somewhat better. |
| ☐ | About the same. |
| ☐ | Somewhat worse. |
| ☐ | Much worse. |
| **What do you think of the staff ?** | |
| ☐ | Kind enough. |
| ☐ | Not so kind. |
| ☐ | Very experienced. |
| ☐ | Need to be trained. |
| **How often do you visit Chen-pi store?** | |
| ☐ | Daily. |
| ☐ | Once a week or more. |
| ☐ | Two or three times per month. |
| ☐ | Several times a year. |
| ☐ | Once a year. |
| ☐ | Other: ________ |
| **What do you suggest us to do urgently to improve our service?** | |
| ☐ | Expand the store. |
| ☐ | Hire more skilled shop assistants. |
| ☐ | Remodel the store. |
| ☐ | Get more items to sell. |

(continued)

| | |
|---|---|
| ☐ | Add after sales services. |
| Do you agree or disagree with the following statements? | |
| ☐ | The window displays are appealing. |
| ☐ | The store is well laid out. |
| ☐ | The signage is clear. |
| ☐ | The signage is informative. |
| ☐ | The store is clean and tidy. |
| ☐ | The store has a pleasant shopping atmosphere. |
| ☐ | The store is easy to move about in. |
| ☐ | There are sufficient checkouts. |

**Assignment 4　SWOT Analysis**

Strengths:

◇The management of Chen-pi store is given the exclusive right to run an Chen-pi special local products store.

◇The store serves the customers who need buy the Jiangmen special local products.

◇The store has extensive contact with the customers, who provide information on the goods needed.

◇The store purchases directly from manufacturers, so it can offer larger discounts to the customers.

◇The rent of the store is for free, because the store is belong to the Palace International.

Weaknesses:

◇The narrow space constrains the store from increasing stock and from offering more services.

◇It is impossible to expand the store at the present location, because the space program of the hotel lobby hasn't been changed till now.

Opportunities:

◇There is only one Chen-pi store which has so full special local products in Jiangmen.

◇There are larges of passenger flow every day in the Palace

International.

◇The number of visitors is growing rapidly due to more and more holiday.

◇More and more tour groups check in the Palace International.

◇There are great number companies nearby.

◇China has already joined the WTO, so it needs qualified personnel to deal with the relevant issues as China becomes more integrated into the world community. The hotel has excellent programs to train such candidates.

◇It is difficult to find a place to buy such full Chen-pi special local products in Jiangmen.

Threats:

◇Many competitors are planning to open such Jiangmen special local products in Jiangmen.

◇The shop assistants are not so experienced, because the hotel always change the employees.

◇Goods prices are getting higher and higher recently. So it is getting more and more difficult to offer discounts to our customers.

◇Online shops that offer discount goods are attracting more and more customers.

### Assignment 5 The action plan

The project will take 8 weeks to implement the project when it has been approved.

| Task | Description | Order/Logic | Time |
|---|---|---|---|
| A | Sign the contract with the hotel. | To be completed first. | Week 1 |
| B | Design the new store layout.<br>Prepare for the remodeling of the new store. | Start when A is completed. | Week 2 |
| C | Start remodeling the store.<br>Order new shelves, equipment and furniture and new goods. | Start when B is completed. | Week 3 |

(continued)

| Task | Description | Order/Logic | Time |
|---|---|---|---|
| D | Hire the new shop assistants.<br>Start training the new shop assistants. | Start when C is completed. | Week 4 |
| E | Check and accept the remodeling project.<br>Publicize on campus store expansion. | Start when D is completed. | Week 5 |
| F | Get the new equipment delivered and installed.<br>Clean the new store and pack up stock in the old store. | Start when E is completed. | Week 6 |
| G | Close the present store and move everything to the new store.<br>Put the old stock on the shelves.<br>Get the new stock delivered and put on the selves. | Start when F is completed. | Week 7 |
| H | Hold the opening ceremony. | Start when G is completed. | Week 8 |

## Assignment 6 The activity flow chart

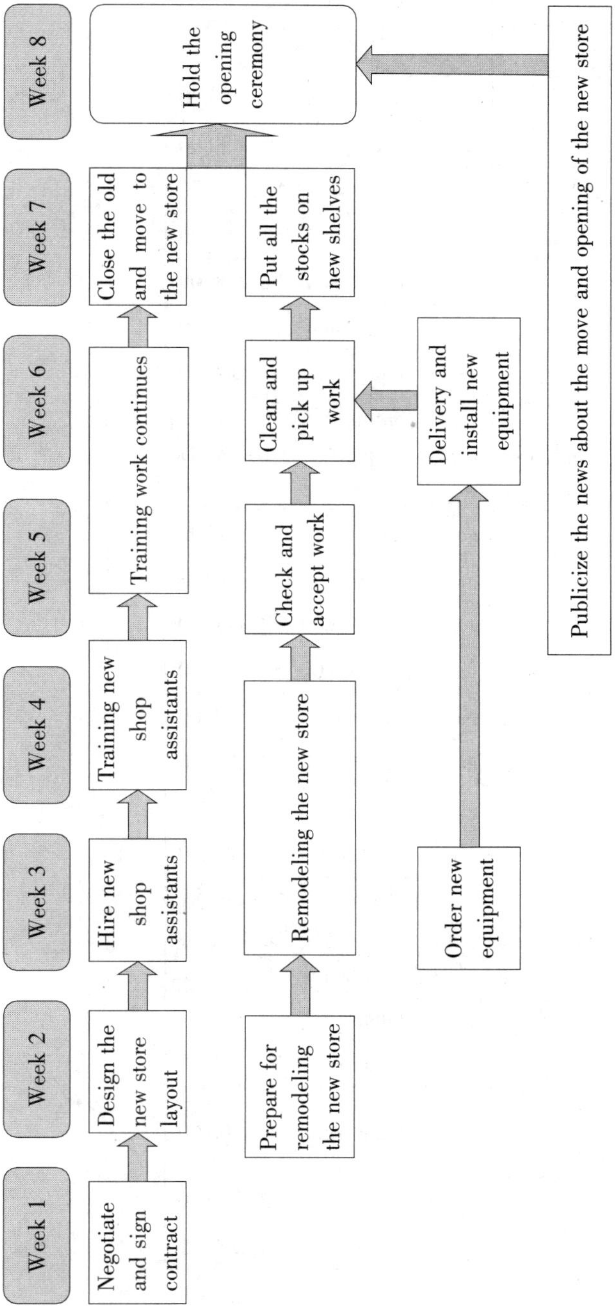

## Assignment 7　Cost breakdown

| Item | Description | Quantity | Unit | Unit Price | Total Cost |
|---|---|---|---|---|---|
| Remodeling | The remodeling costs for the new store would be RMB67, 500 as shown in the following: | | | | |
| 1 | Labor costs | | | Lump sum | 48, 000.00 |
| 2 | Flooring | 100 | $m^2$ | ¥50.00 | ¥5, 000.00 |
| 3 | Paint | 200 | kg | ¥10.00 | ¥2, 000.00 |
| 4 | Lumber | | | Lump sum | ¥1, 500.00 |
| 5 | Lighting | | | Lump sum | ¥8, 000.00 |
| 6 | Glue & tools | | | Lump sum | ¥2, 000.00 |
| 7 | Cement & putty | 6 | ton | Lump sum | ¥1, 000.00 |
| | | | | Sub-total: | ¥67, 500.00 |
| Equipment | The cost of equipment in the new bookshop would be RMB38, 800 as shown in the following: | | | | |
| 1 | Photocopier | 1 | ea | ¥3, 500.00 | ¥3, 500.00 |
| 2 | Shelves | 500 | ea | ¥30.00 | ¥15, 000.00 |
| 3 | Office furniture | 1 | set | ¥3, 000.00 | ¥3, 000.00 |
| 4 | Computers | 2 | ea | ¥4, 500.00 | ¥9, 000.00 |
| 5 | Printers | 2 | ea | ¥1, 500.00 | ¥3, 000.00 |
| 6 | Air conditioners | 2 | ea | ¥2, 000.00 | ¥4, 000.00 |
| 7 | Armchairs | 3 | ea | ¥100.00 | ¥300.00 |
| 8 | Office supplies | 1 | set | ¥1, 000.00 | ¥1, 000.00 |
| | | | | Sub-total: | ¥38, 800.00 |
| Budget | The annual increase in the operating budget would be RMB35, 300 as shown in the following: | | | | |
| 1 | Wages | | | Lump sum | ¥28, 000.00 |
| 2 | Utilities | | | Lump sum | ¥3, 000.00 |
| 3 | Equipment maintenance | | | Lump sum | ¥1, 500.00 |
| 4 | Consultant fees | | | Lump sum | ¥2, 800.00 |
| | | | | Sub-total: | ¥35, 300.00 |

(continued)

| Total cost of the whole project = Initial costs + Recurrent costs = RMB106, 300 as shown in the following: | | | | | |
|---|---|---|---|---|---|
| Initial costs | Remodeling | | | Lump sum | ¥67, 500.00 |
| | Equipment | | | Lump sum | ¥70, 300.00 |
| | | | | Sub-total: | ¥137,800.00 |
| Recurrent costs | Rental | | Mon | Lump sum | ¥5, 000.00 |
| | Operating budget | | | Lump sum | ¥35, 000.00 |
| | | | | Sub-total: | ¥40, 000.00 |
| | | | | Total: | ¥191, 300.00 |

### Assignment 8 Risk analysis

Before putting the plan into practice, the manager finds that the following problems might affect the successful completion of the project. These problems, also called risks, generally fall into three categories.

People-related:

◇The new employees may not good at selling goods at all.

◇Some customers may pilfer from the Chen-pi store.

◇The clerks next door may not happy with the noises resulting from the remodeling of the new site and may demand no remodeling during the working hours.

Time-related:

◇The university may shorten the period of the lease of the new site and even worse, expropriate the new store.

Product-related:

◇The loan may not be obtained from the bank in time.

◇The paint applied to the walls may not live up to the quality and begin to fall off shortly after the decoration.

◇The new stock may not cater to the interests of the customer.

Since it's impossible to eradicate all these risks, the store manager thinks he has to control and manage them. Now, he has thought of three measures.

◇Try to avoid the risks, i.e. to prevent the dangers from

happening, say, carrying out market research among target customers to improve the popularity of the stock and remaining constant contact with the instructors to get the latest information of textbooks.

◇Prepare alternatives beforehand in case the dangers actually happen, say, contacting more clerk candidates as substitutes in case the employed are not qualified and trying to finish the remodeling within the weekends if the dissatisfaction occurred from the neighboring clerks.

◇Set aside a certain percentage of the total budget as contingency allowance to take account of the unexpected risks, such as to cover the pilferage loss and to cover the re-painting expense.

After the risk analysis, we think three more items should be added to the total costs:

| | |
|---|---|
| Public relations | 2, 000 yuan per annum |
| Market research | 1, 000 yuan per annum |
| Contingency allowance | 1% of the annual profit |

So that would be: RMB 315, 600+3, 000+1% of the annual profit.

Student's Practice 2
(新建项目实例)

# Proposal for Setting up Water Flower Bra Shop

Submitted to Mr. Smith
General Manager
West Branch of Bank of China

Prepared by Joan Chen
Sales Manager
Friendship Store

Tel：1362288××××
Fax：86-0750-370××××
E-mail：joanchen@126.com
Date：Apr. 25th, 2015

# Table of Contents

## Abstract

The Water Flower Bra Shop plans to set up in the center of Jiangmen city as a leaguer shop of Water Flower Bra. It will locate in Gangkou Road. The bra shop will take up about 25 square meters, its main business is selling bras, underwear, evening gown set, fitness wear, etc. After the shop is set up, the project will bring to us net profit about RMB8,000 per month.

The bra shop needs at least RMB80, 000 to start the business, including shop rent, fitment, first batch of minimum purchase, joining the brand, labor, as well as furniture, air conditioners and shelves for exhibition, etc. The whole project will be completed within two months according to the timetable. The new shop will definitely attract the customers soon.

The shop is privately owned with a new brand in Jiangmen city. In fact, this brand has already been well-known in Shanghai and other large cities for its good quality and fashionable styles. It will become popular in Jiangmen soon. On the other hand, with the development of the society, people are getting more and more interested in cultural life, they will tend to ask for some products with well-known brands. Besides, the price is not so high that the ladies in Jiangmen would surely accept it.

The general objective of the project is to promote the brand and make profit as much as possible.

## I. Introduction

The Water Flower Bra Shop will set up in the center of Jiangmen city, it will locate in Gangkou Road, opposite to Donghu Park. The shop will be about 25 square meters of the total size.

The Water Flower Bra Shop is privately owned. Its main business is selling bras, underwear, evening gown set, fitness wear, etc. for ladies who are working, living and shopping around there.

In order to get approval of the project and get a clearer idea and opinions of the customers, three focus groups were organized to investigate the customers' satisfaction and dissatisfaction. According to the market survey, we get some complaints from customers about the sellers lacking of knowledge, lacking discounts, and fitting room. Through the survey, we get some good suggestions for the business, such as to hire sellers with more experience, provide more discounts, and provide a ventilated fitting room, and so on.

The bra shop needs at least RMB80, 000 to start the business, the rent, fitment, purchase products, shelves and other furniture. The income from sales per month is expected to be about RMB8,000 of the net profit, that is RMB96, 000 per year. In one year, it could generally regain the investment. From the next year on, we will be able to pay off the loan and begin to get profit.

## Ⅱ. The Body

### Part 1 Findings and Analysis

### 1.1 Current Business Analysis

#### 1.1.1 Analysis of the business

The Water Flower Bra Shop plans to set up in the centre of Jiangmen city as the league shop of Water Flower Bra. It will locate in Gangkou Road. It will be about 25 square meters of the total size. Near the bra shop is the high-class office building Zhongyuan building, the well-known park Donghu Park, McDonald's and KFC. There are lots of consumers around there. With the development of this society, people become more and more interested in cultural life, they will tend to ask for some products with well-known brands.

The new shop would cost about RMB2, 000 for the rent per month. The fitment of the shop will be about RMB20, 000. The fee for the first batch of minimum purchase will be RMB15,000; the fund for joining the brand is RMB3, 000, The labor cost is about RMB2,000 per month; water and electricity about RMB200 per month. At least RMB80, 000 is needed to start the business.

Investment repayment: after the bra shop getting on the track, the income from sales per month (net-profit) will be about RMB 8, 000, about a year later, it will generally regain investment.

The main business of the bra shop is selling bras, underwear, evening gown set, fitness wear, etc.

### 1.1.2 Customer profile

The majority of the customers of the shop are the office ladies near the shop, because their offices are near the shop. When they go to work or come off duty, they will pass through the shop and the shop will catch their eyes. As long as we get one of those customers, the others will get known of the shop too, as they will talk about the shop during work at office. They account for 50 percent of the customers.

The residents living near the shop. They account for 30 percents of the customers. Residents who live near Gangkou Road mostly are rich persons, and they usually request high-class quality and well-known brands.

People from other regions, such as tourists, visitors. Gangkou Road is one of the shopping centers in Jiangmen, most of the citizens would like to go to Gangkou Road for shopping.

### 1.2 Focus Group Minutes

In order to get approval of the project, three focus groups were organized. The focus groups were as follows:

◇10 office ladies around the place the shop will be located.

◇10 local residents.

◇10 ladies who often go shopping nearby.

◇5 girls aged 18 – 20.

◇5 women aged 40 – 50.

Since each of the mentioned categories of customer might have different expectations, views and needs, separate focus groups would be desirable.

Anyhow, a basic list of questions was prepared beforehand, but the discussions with each focus group were allowed to be free and open. Questions prepared are:

◇Do you know the brand of Water Flower?

◇If yes, what do you think of Water Flower?

◇What do you think of bra?

◇What price could you accept?

◇How many bras do you buy each year?

◇Which brand do you know?

◇Which brand are you wearing now?

◇What do you expect the shop to be when it opens?

◇Do you have any suggestions for a bra shop?

Complaints gathered from the focus groups are:

◇The sellers haven't had enough knowledge of bra.

◇Most of the shops do not provide enough discounts.

◇Some bra shops do not provide a fitting room.

Their suggestions are:

◇Hire sellers with more experience.

◇Provide more discounts, especially during some festivals and special days.

◇Provide a ventilated fitting room.

## 1.3 Customer Surveys Design

| **Water Flower Bra Shop** | | | | | |
|---|---|---|---|---|---|
| **Customer Survey**<br>Water Flower Bra shop is committed to customer satisfaction and would like to know customers' expectations. Your answers will help us to identify what we should do to set up this shop. If you have questions about this survey, please contact Joan Chen (0750-3701557). Thank you for your time and suggestions. | | | | | |
| What is your overall satisfaction with bra you ever bought from the stores around? | | | | | |
| | 5<br>(Very satisfied) | 4 | 3 | 2 | 1<br>(Very dissatisfied) |
| | □ | □ | □ | □ | □ |
| How satisfied are you with the following areas of the stores around? | | | | | |
| | 5<br>(Very satisfied) | 4 | 3 | 2 | 1<br>(Very dissatisfied) |
| The space | □ | □ | □ | □ | □ |
| The price | □ | □ | □ | □ | □ |
| Quality | □ | □ | □ | □ | □ |
| Business hours | □ | □ | □ | □ | □ |
| Ability to meet customers' needs | □ | □ | □ | □ | □ |

(continued)

| How satisfied are you with the environment of the stores around? | | | | | |
|---|---|---|---|---|---|
| | 5 (Very satisfied) | 4 | 3 | 2 | 1 (Very dissatisfied) |
| The lighting | ☐ | ☐ | ☐ | ☐ | ☐ |
| The color of the chest | ☐ | ☐ | ☐ | ☐ | ☐ |
| The ventilation | ☐ | ☐ | ☐ | ☐ | ☐ |
| The inner decoration | ☐ | ☐ | ☐ | ☐ | ☐ |
| The outer look | ☐ | ☐ | ☐ | ☐ | ☐ |

| What do you think of the services provided by the stores around? | |
|---|---|
| ☐ | Very good. |
| ☐ | Good. |
| ☐ | Not so good. |
| ☐ | Bad. |
| ☐ | Too bad. |

| What do you think of the staff? | |
|---|---|
| ☐ | Kind enough. |
| ☐ | Not so kind. |
| ☐ | Very experienced. |
| ☐ | Need to be trained. |

| How often do you visit bra stores? | |
|---|---|
| ☐ | Daily. |
| ☐ | Once a week or more. |
| ☐ | Two or three times per month. |
| ☐ | Several times a year. |
| ☐ | Once a year. |
| ☐ | Other: ________ |

| What do you suggest us to do urgently to set up our shop? | |
|---|---|
| ☐ | Get a site large enough. |
| ☐ | Hire enough skilled shop assistants. |
| ☐ | Remodel the store comfortably. |
| ☐ | Get more items to sell. |
| ☐ | Add after sales services. |

(continued)

| Do you agree or disagree with the following statements? | |
|---|---|
| ☐ | The shop is going to be located downtown. |
| ☐ | The shop is to be well laid out. |
| ☐ | The assistants are to be beautiful young girls. |
| ☐ | The signage is informative. |
| ☐ | The shop is clean and tidy inside. |
| ☐ | The shop has a pleasant shopping atmosphere. |
| ☐ | The shop is easy to move about. |
| ☐ | There are only two checkouts. |

### 1.4 SWOT Analysis

Strengths:

◇The shop is to be located in the center of the city, where people like to go shopping there.

◇The suppliers will offer the staff a training course.

◇The suppliers will provide some presents for promotion and provide the clients with VIP cards.

◇Easy to return 100% of the goods of poor quality to the suppliers and get the exchange for the new.

◇Stock is directly from the suppliers, thus we could provide more discount to clients.

Weaknesses:

◇It's hard to hire well-trained staff with good experience.

◇The brand is still not so popular in Jiangmen city.

◇There are lots of bras with cheaper prices in Jiangmen city.

◇There are lots of other bra brands in Jiangmen city, and the competition is fierce.

Opportunities:

◇High-class office buildings are around there, and the office ladies are around there too.

◇Lots of ladies like to go shopping and play around there.

◇Residents are increasing around there.

Threats:

◇There are lots of bra shops in Jiangmen city, competition is sure to be very intense.

◇Online shops are rapidly increased, they become more and more attractive to people.

◇Lots of bras are with cheaper prices.

◇Lots of well-known brands in Jiangmen city.

## Part 2 Planning the Activities

### 2. 1 The Action Plan

Our project will begin immediately after it is approved and the budget is available. It will take about two months to implement the project. Here is the action plan table for reference:

| Task | Description | Order/Logic | Time |
|---|---|---|---|
| A | Sign the contract with the proprietor. | To be completed first. | Week 1 |
| B | Design the new store layout.<br>Prepare for the remodeling of the new store. | Start when A is completed. | Week 2 |
| C | Start remodeling the shop.<br>Order new shelves, equipment and furniture and new goods.<br>Hire the shop assistants. | Start when B is completed. | Week 3 |
| D | Start training the new shop assistants. | Start when C is completed. | Week 4 |
| E | Check and accept the remodeling project.<br>Publicize on the setting up the Water Flower Bra Shop. | Start when D is completed. | Week 5 |
| F | Get the new equipment delivered and installed.<br>Clean the new store. | Start when E is completed. | Week 6 |
| G | Put the old stock on the shelves.<br>Get the new stock delivered and put on the shelves. | Start when F is completed. | Week 7 |
| H | Hold the opening ceremony. | Start when G is completed. | Week 8 |

## 2. 2 The Activity Flow Chart

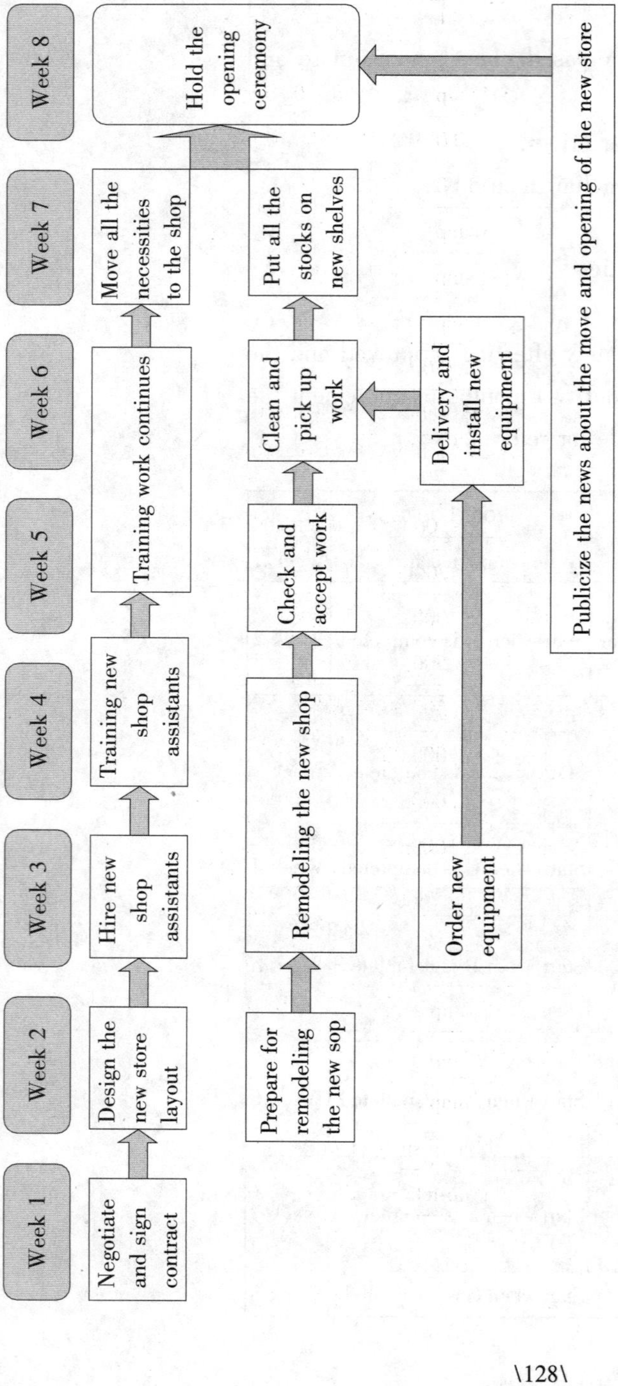

### 2. 3 Cost Breakdown

| Item | Description | Quantity | Unit | Unit Price | Total Cost |
|---|---|---|---|---|---|
| Remodeling | The remodeling costs for the new store would be RMB84,500.00 as shown in the following: | | | | |
| 1 | Labor costs | | | Lump sum | ¥50, 000.00 |
| 2 | Flooring | 100 | $m^2$ | ¥50.00 | ¥16, 000.00 |
| 3 | Paint | 200 | kg | ¥10.00 | ¥4, 000.00 |
| 4 | Lumber | | | Lump sum | ¥1, 500.00 |
| 5 | lighting | | | Lump sum | ¥8, 000.00 |
| 6 | Ceilings | | | Lump sum | ¥3, 000.00 |
| 7 | Cement & putty | 5 | ton | ¥400.00 | ¥2, 000.00 |
| | | | | Sub-total: | ¥84, 500.00 |
| Equipment | The cost of equipment in the new bookshop would be RMB70, 300 as shown in the following: | | | | |
| 1 | Exhibition cupboard | 2 | ea | ¥15, 000.00 | ¥30, 000.00 |
| 2 | Exhibition shelf | 3 | ea | ¥10, 000.00 | ¥30, 000.00 |
| 3 | Office furniture | 1 | set | ¥3, 000.00 | ¥3, 000.00 |
| 4 | Computers | 2 | ea | ¥4, 500.00 | ¥9, 000.00 |
| 5 | Printers | 2 | ea | ¥1, 500.00 | ¥3, 000.00 |
| 6 | Air conditioners | 3 | ea | ¥2, 000.00 | ¥6, 000.00 |
| 7 | Sofa | 5 | ea | ¥1, 000.00 | ¥5, 000.00 |
| 8 | Office supplies | 1 | set | ¥1, 000.00 | ¥1, 000.00 |
| | | | | Sub-total: | ¥87, 000.00 |
| Budget: | The annual increase in the operating budget would be RMB35, 300 as shown in the following: | | | | |
| 1 | Wages | | | Lump sum | ¥35, 000.00 |
| 2 | Utilities | | | Lump sum | ¥4, 000.00 |
| 3 | Equipment maintenance | | | Lump sum | ¥2, 000.00 |
| 4 | Consultant fees | | | Lump sum | ¥5, 000.00 |
| | | | | Sub-total: | ¥46, 000.00 |

(continued)

| Total cost of the whole project = Initial costs + Recurrent costs = RMB173, 100 as shown in the following: | | | | | |
|---|---|---|---|---|---|
| Initial costs | Remodeling | | | Lump sum | ¥84, 000.00 |
| | Equipment | | | Lump sum | ¥87,000.00 |
| | | | | Sub-total: | ¥171,000.00 |
| Recurrent costs | Rental | | | Lump sum | ¥60, 000.00 |
| | Operating budget | | | Lump sum | ¥50, 000.00 |
| | | | | Sub-total: | ¥110,000.00 |
| | | | | Total: | 498, 500.00 |

## 2. 4 Risk Analysis & Management

Before we put the plan into practice, the management finds that the following risks might affect the successful completion of the project. These risks generally fall into three categories.

People-related:

◇The employees to be hired may not be good at selling bras at all.

◇Some customers may feel shy to go into the bra shop.

◇The owner next door may not be so happy with the noises resulting from the remodeling of the site and may ask for no remodeling during the working hours.

Time-related:

◇The proprietor may shorten the period of the lease of the site and even worse, expropriate the new store in a short time.

◇The newly ordered equipment may not arrive in time, causing delay in the opening of the new store.

Product-related:

◇The loan may not be obtained from the bank or not in time.

◇The paint applied to the walls may not live up to the quality and begin to fall off shortly after the decoration.

◇The stock may not cater to the interests of the customer.

Now that it's impossible to eliminate all these risks, the shop owner thinks she has to control and manage them. And she has come up with four measures:

◇Try to prevent the risks from happening by carrying out market research among target customers to improve the popularity of the stock and remaining constant contact with the instructors to get the latest information of products.

◇Prepare alternatives beforehand in case the risks actually happen by contacting more clerk candidates as substitutes in case the employed are not qualified.

◇Try to finish the remodeling within the weekends if the dissatisfaction occurred from the neighboring clerks.

◇Set aside a certain percentage of the total budget as contingency allowance to take account of the unexpected risks, such as to cover the pilferage loss and to cover the repainting expense.

After the risk analysis, we think three more items should be added to the total costs:

| | |
|---|---|
| Public relations | 5, 000 yuan per year |
| Market research | 8, 000 yuan per year |
| Contingency allowance | 1% of the annual profit |

So the total cost of the project would be: RMB498, 000.00 + 13, 000+1% of the annual profit .

## Ⅲ. Conclusion

In conclusion, I firmly believe that the project will be successful. As Water Flower is a Hong Kong company, it is able to produce good-quality products with fashionable styles and various colors. Though the manager has got only few years' experience in doing such a business, yet she is determined to get this brand popular soon in this city and make it quite attractive to most of the ladies in Jiangmen. As one of the league shops of Water Flower, and the only one in Jiangmen city, the shop will surely make profit and could enlarge the business soon.

It will be highly appreciated if you could read this proposal and be so kind as to offer me some good ideas. I do hope we could have a chance to discuss this plan and make it more feasible with your help and guide. Please feel free and contact me at any time. I'll be always ready to meet with you.

## Ⅳ. Bibliography

[1] John Hilton，羡锡彪. 实用商务项目设计. 北京：中央广播电视大学出版社，2001.

[2] Mary Ellen Guffey. 国际商务交际. 北京：中央广播电视大学出版社，2004.

[3] http://www.project.com

[4] http://www.budiniss.uk

[5] http://www.statistics.gov.

## V. Appendix

### Assignment 1  Analysis of the business

Water Flower Bra Shop plans to set up in the centre of Jiangmen city as the league shop of Water Flower Bra. It will locate in Gangkou Road. It will be about 25 square meters of the total size. Near the bra shop is the high-class office building Zhongyuan Building, the well-known park Donghu Park, McDonald' s and KFC. There are lots of consumers around there. With the development of this society, people become more and more interested in cultural life, they will tend to ask for some products with well-known brands.

The new shop would cost about RMB 2,000 for the rent per month. The fitment of the shop will be about RMB 20,000. The fee for the first batch of minimum purchase will be RMB 15,000; the fund for joining the brand is RMB 3, 000. The labor costs about RMB 2,000 per month; water and electricity about RMB 200 per month. At least RMB 80, 000 is needed to start the business.

Investment repayment: After the bra shop getting on the track, the income from sales per month (net-profit) will be about RMB 8,000 , about a year later, it will generally regain the investment.

The main business of the bra shop is selling bras, underwear, evening gown set, fitness wear, etc.

### Assignment 2 Focus group minutes

In order to get approval of the project, three focus groups were organized. The focus groups were as follows:

◇10 office ladies around the shop.

◇10 residents.

◇10 ladies who were shopping around the shop.

We have prepared the following questions for the focus group:

◇Do you know the brand of Water Flower?

◇If yes, what do you think of Water Flower?

◇What do you think of bra?

◇What price could you accept?

◇How many bras would you like to buy each year?

◇What brand do you know?

◇What brand are you using now?

◇What do you expect the shop to be when it opens?

◇Do you have any suggestions for a bra shop?

The comlpaints we've got from the focus groups are as follow:

◇The sellers haven't had enough knowledge of bra.

◇Most of the shops did not provide enough discounts.

◇Some bra shops could not provide a fitting room.

The suggestions we've got are:

◇Hire sellers with more experience.

◇Provide more discounts, especially during some festivals or special days.

◇Provide a ventilated fitting room.

| Water Flower Bra Shop | | | | |
|---|---|---|---|---|
| **Customer Survey**<br>Water Flower Bra shop is committed to customers' satisfaction and would like to know customers' expectations. Your answers will help us to identify what we should do to set up this shop. If you have questions about this survey, please contact Joan Chen (0750–3701557). Thank you for your time and suggestions. | | | | |
| What is your overall satisfaction with bra you ever bought from the stores around? | | | | |
| | 5 (Very satisfied) | 4 | 3 | 2 | 1 (Very dissatisfied) |
| | ☐ | ☐ | ☐ | ☐ | ☐ |
| How satisfied are you with the following areas of the stores around? | | | | | |
| | 5 (Very satisfied) | 4 | 3 | 2 | 1 (Very dissatisfied) |
| The space | ☐ | ☐ | ☐ | ☐ | ☐ |
| The price | ☐ | ☐ | ☐ | ☐ | ☐ |
| Quality | ☐ | ☐ | ☐ | ☐ | ☐ |
| Business hours | ☐ | ☐ | ☐ | ☐ | ☐ |
| Ability to meet customers' needs | ☐ | ☐ | ☐ | ☐ | ☐ |
| How satisfied are you with the environment of the stores around? | | | | | |
| | 5 (Very satisfied) | 4 | 3 | 2 | 1 (Very dissatisfied) |
| The lighting | ☐ | ☐ | ☐ | ☐ | ☐ |
| The color of the chest | ☐ | ☐ | ☐ | ☐ | ☐ |
| The ventilation | ☐ | ☐ | ☐ | ☐ | ☐ |
| The inner decoration | ☐ | ☐ | ☐ | ☐ | ☐ |
| The outer look | ☐ | ☐ | ☐ | ☐ | ☐ |
| What do you think of the services provided by the stores around? | | | | | |
| ☐ | Very good. | | | | |
| ☐ | Good. | | | | |
| ☐ | Not so good. | | | | |
| ☐ | Bad. | | | | |
| ☐ | Too bad. | | | | |

(continued)

## Assignment 3 Customer surveys design

| | |
|---|---|
| What do you think of the staff? | |
| ☐ | Kind enough. |
| ☐ | Not so kind. |
| ☐ | Very experienced. |
| ☐ | Need to be trained. |
| How often do you visit bra stores? | |
| ☐ | Daily. |
| ☐ | Once a week or more. |
| ☐ | Two or three times per month. |
| ☐ | Several times a year. |
| ☐ | Once a year |
| ☐ | Other: ________________ |
| What do you suggest us to do urgently to set up our shop? | |
| ☐ | Get a site large enough. |
| ☐ | Hire enough skilled shop assistants. |
| ☐ | Remodel the store comfortably. |
| ☐ | Get more items to sell. |
| ☐ | Add after sales services. |
| Do you agree or disagree with the following statements? | |
| ☐ | The shop is going to be located downtown. |
| ☐ | The shop is to be well laid out. |
| ☐ | The assistants are to be beautiful young girls. |
| ☐ | The signage is informative. |
| ☐ | The shop is clean and tidy inside. |
| ☐ | The shop has a pleasant shopping atmosphere. |
| ☐ | The shop is easy to move about. |
| ☐ | There are only two checkouts. |

**Assignment 4 SWOT analysis**

Strengths:

◇The shop is in the center of the city, and people like to go shopping there.

◇The suppliers will offer the staff a training course.

◇The suppliers will provide some presents for promotion and provide the clients with VIP cards.

◇Easy to return 100% of the goods of poor quality to the suppliers and get the exchange for the new.

◇Stock is directly from the suppliers, thus we could provide more discounts to clients.

Weaknesses:

◇It's hard to hire well-trained staff with good experience.

◇The brand is still not so popular in Jiangmen city.

◇There are lots of bras with cheap price in Jiangmen city.

◇There are lots of other brands in Jiangmen , and the competition is fierce.

Opportunities:

◇High-class office buildings are around there, where office ladies are around there too.

◇Lots of ladies like to go shopping and play around there.

◇Residents are getting more and more around there.

Threats:

◇There are lots of bra shops in Jiangmen city, and the competition is sure to be very great.

◇Online shops are rapidly increased, they become more and more attractive to people.

◇Lots of bras are with cheap price.

◇There are lots of well-known brands in Jiangmen city.

## Assignment 5 The action plan

| Task | Description | Order/Logic | Time |
|---|---|---|---|
| A | Sign the contract with the landlord. | To be completed first. | Week 1 |
| B | Design the new store layout.<br>Prepare for the remodeling of the new store. | Start when A is completed. | Week 2 |
| C | Start remodeling the shop.<br>Order new shelves, equipment and furniture and new goods. | Start when B is completed. | Week 3 |
| D | Hire the shop assistants.<br>Start training the new shop assistants. | Start when C is completed. | Week 4 |
| E | Check and accept the remodeling project.<br>Publicize on the setting up Water Flower Bra Shop. | Start when D is completed. | Week 5 |
| F | Get the new equipment delivered and installed.<br>Clean the new store. | Start when E is completed. | Week 6 |
| G | Put the old stock on the shelves.<br>Get the new stock delivered and put on the selves. | Start when F is completed. | Week 7 |
| H | Hold the opening ceremony. | Start when G is completed. | Week 8 |

## Assignment 6 The activity flow chart

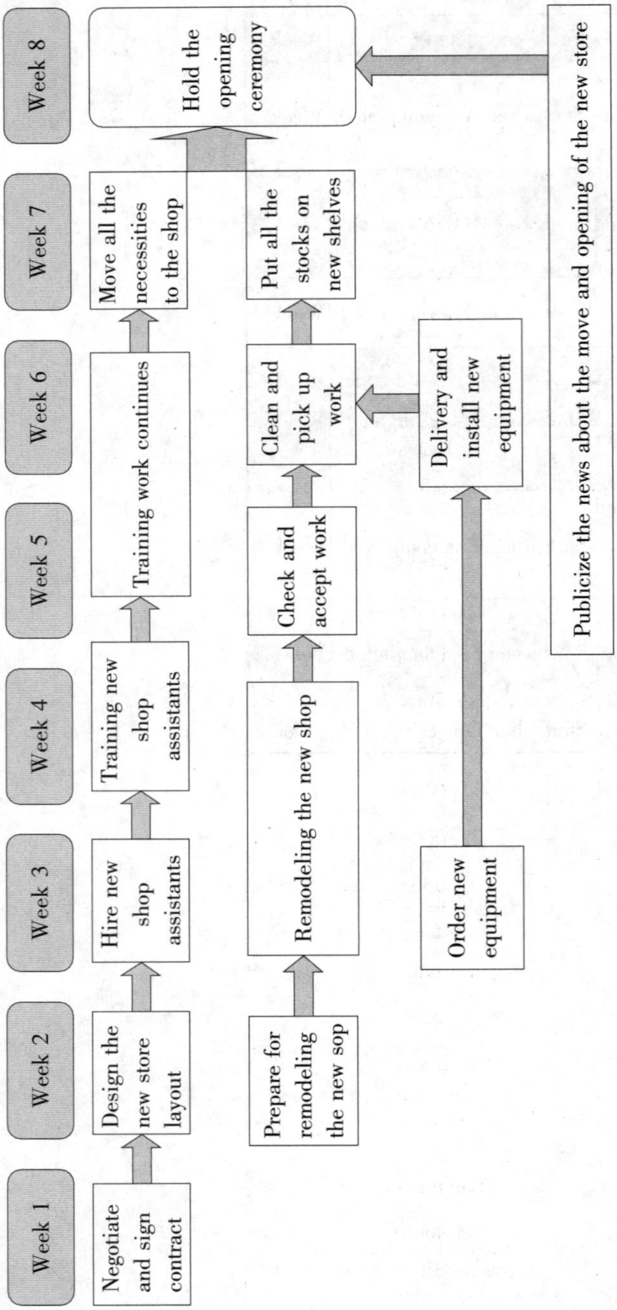

## Assignment 7　Cost breakdown

| Item | Description | Quantity | Unit | Unit Price | Total Cost |
|---|---|---|---|---|---|
| Remodeling | The remodeling costs for the new store would be RMB84,000,00 as shown in the following: | | | | |
| 1 | Labor costs | | | Lump sum | ¥50, 000.00 |
| 3 | Flooring | 100 | m² | ¥50.00 | ¥16, 000.00 |
| 4 | Paint | 200 | kg | ¥10.00 | ¥4, 000.00 |
| 6 | Lumber | | | Lump sum | ¥1, 500.00 |
| 7 | Lighting | | | Lump sum | ¥8, 000.00 |
| 8 | Ceilings | | | Lump sum | ¥3, 000.00 |
| 9 | Cement & putty | 6 | ton | Lump sum | ¥2, 000.00 |
| | | | | Sub-total: | ¥84, 000.00 |
| Equipment | The cost of equipment in the new bookshop would be RMB70, 300 as shown in the following: | | | | |
| 1 | Exhibition cupboard | 2 | ea | ¥15, 000.00 | ¥30, 000.00 |
| 2 | Exhibition shelf | 3 | ea | ¥10, 000.00 | ¥30, 000.00 |
| 3 | Office furniture | 1 | set | ¥3, 000.00 | ¥3, 000.00 |
| 4 | Computers | 2 | ea | ¥4, 500.00 | ¥9, 000.00 |
| 5 | Printers | 2 | ea | ¥1, 500.00 | ¥3, 000.00 |
| 6 | Air conditioners | 3 | ea | ¥2, 000.00 | ¥6, 000.00 |
| 7 | Sofa | 5 | ea | ¥1, 000.00 | ¥5, 000.00 |
| 8 | Office supplies | 1 | set | ¥2, 000.00 | ¥1, 000.00 |
| | | | | Sub-total: | ¥87, 000.00 |
| Budget | The annual increase in the operating budget would be RMB35, 300 as shown in the following: | | | | |
| 1 | Wages | | | Lump sum | ¥35, 000.00 |
| 2 | Utilities | | | Lump sum | ¥4, 000.00 |
| 3 | Equipment maintenance | | | Lump sum | ¥2, 000.00 |
| 4 | Consultant fees | | | Lump sum | ¥5, 000.00 |
| | | | | Sub-total: | ¥46, 000.00 |
| Total cost of the whole project = Initial costs + Recurrent costs = RMB173, 100 as shown in the following: | | | | | |

(continued)

| | | | | | |
|---|---|---|---|---|---|
| Initial costs | Remodeling | | | Lump sum | ¥84,000.00 |
| | Equipment | | | Lump sum | ¥87,000.00 |
| | | | | Sub-total: | ¥171,000.00 |
| Recurrent costs | Rental | | | Lump sum | ¥60,000.00 |
| | Operating budget | | | Lump sum | ¥50,000.00 |
| | | | | Sub-total: | ¥110,000.00 |
| | | | | Total: | ¥498,000.00 |

**Assignment 8 Risk analysis**

Through the business analysis, we have found some potential risks in the project:

◇There are lots of bra shops in Jiangmen city, and the competition is large.

◇Online shops are rapidly increased, they become more and more attractive to people.

◇Lots of bras are of cheap price.

◇There are lots of well-known brands in Jiangmen city.

◇The shop staff are lack of experience.

It's impossible to get rid of all those risks, but we are able to take some measures to avoid some:

◇Train the staff regularly.

◇Provide more discounts or prompt sales, especially in festivals.

◇Persuade the suppliers to do more advertisement.

# Appendix Two

★任务驱动式学习指导建议

对商务英语专业方向的学生而言，毕业项目设计即商务项目设计；对旅游英语专业方向的学生来说，毕业项目设计则是模拟旅游项目开发或旅游市场调查报告。前者是对一个商务项目的可行性进行调查研究与分析，确定实施该项目并撰写项目计划书，比如通过以计划书的形式说明项目的可行性以及利润前景，使老板、合资人或银行同意为该项目提供资金或贷款，也可出资合作该项目。具体地说，假设学生想在某地开一家书店，但资金不够，需要融资100万元人民币，于是学生必须撰写一份项目计划书来说服银行或自己的目标合伙人贷款或出资。学生在正式撰写计划书之前，须完成的具体任务有：①商业分析/市场分析；②核心小组座谈；③问卷调查表设计；④SWOT分析；⑤项目实施计划表；⑥项目实施流程图；⑦成本核算；⑧风险分析。最终学生根据以上的资料用英文写出相应的商务项目计划书。后者则是让学生假设以当地政府为说服对象，就当地的某个旅游资源项目开发的可行性进行调查研究与分析，通过实地考察掌握第一手资料。具体任务有：①开展旅游市场调查分析；②核心小组座谈；③问卷调查表设计；④SWOT分析；⑤项目实施具体计划；⑥项目实施流程图；⑦成本核算；⑧风险分析。最终学生根据以上的资料用英文撰写出相应的旅游项目开发计划书。

★写作的基本原则与要求建议

模拟商务项目设计必须依据商务实践各个环节的活动内容进行分析总结，尽可能以毕业顶岗实习单位为模拟对象，遵循真实性的原则。项目运作和论文报告要体现出SMART的要求（specific, measurable, agreed, realistic and time-bound，即明确性、可评估性、一致性、真实性和时限性）。

要求学生能以严谨的学风、科学的方法、实事求是的态度和勇于创新的精神来完成项目设计全过程。在正式写作之前，指导教师应对学生的项目设计选题严格把关，对不符合要求与现实情况的选题一律不得同意开题。每一位指导老师对项目设计的具体要求、项目的启动、问题的分析方式、方案的设计原则、数据的收集方式、问卷调查的设计、数据的分析以及项目设计中各部分的撰写规范等可以进行集中指导，但对于每一位学生的方案设计、八大分项作业以及最终计划书的撰写等，指导教师可以采用比较灵活的个别指导方式，尤其是可以进行网络在线指导。

通常情况下，要求每一位参加毕业设计的学生独立完成上述的八大分项任务，并完成最终计划书的撰写，但也可以根据各院校自身的实际情况采取以项目小组为单位协同完成。项目小组以4～6人为宜。据了解，番禺职业技术学院、江门职业技术学院就采取这种方式，反响良好，这不但可以培养学生独立思考和动手的能力，又可以培养学生的团队协作意识，还减轻了师生双方的任务强度。

★关于选题的建议

选题不宜过大，如“广东西江流域水质污染治理计划书”、“珠江三角洲外贸企业发展计划书”等题目，显然过大，非一般人所能完成；反之，题目也不可太小，如“2009年除夕家庭聚会计划书”“班级英语角活动场所扩展计划书”等，这些题目只涉及家庭或班集体，并非商务项目设计要解决的问题。总而言之，对大项目要力求具体而明确，如“创建微燕综合贸易公司计划书”；小项目要力求具有延伸性或扩展性。选题要考虑项目设计的可操作性和现实性，以及由计划书选题可能带来的各种相关因素。选题不必局限于社会商务活动，凡是涉及投入和产出的项目，并且获得相关授权（主要是指有些需要匿名的商业机密项目）的项目，都可以作为选题的范围。以下是部分选题示例，作为参照：

（一）新建项目类

1. Proposal for Setting up Future-star Kids' Book Store
（创建未来之星儿童书店计划书）

2. Proposal for Setting up East Training Centre of Self-taught

Exams

（创办东方自学考试培训中心计划书）

3. Proposal for Developing Temple of Gao's into Tourist Attraction

（开发旅游景点高家祠堂计划书）

（二）扩建项目类

1. Proposal for School Book Bar Expansion

（校园书吧扩建计划书）

2. Proposal for the Expansion of Brothers Appliance Equipment Company

（兄弟电器设备公司扩展计划书）

3. Proposal for the Expansion of Guifeng Mountain Resort

（圭峰山度假村扩建计划书）

（三）其他类

1. Proposal for Afforestation of Jiangmen City

（江门城市绿化计划书）

2. Proposal for Pre-post Training of Ligong Hotel New Staff

（丽宫酒店新职员岗前培训计划书）

3. Proposal for Promotion of Touring Products

（旅游产品促销计划书）

以上选题仅供参考。学生应根据各自的具体情况另拟新的题目。注意各班在选题时应尽量避免重复。

★考核建议

首先由指导老师根据学生完成以上项目的设计与实施的具体情况（项目设计与实施过程占60%，项目计划书占40%）及项目计划书的写作质量（五个等级：优秀、良好、中等、及格、不及格）来评定总成绩，并对项目计划书正文及附件作出评语。毕业项目设计成绩由本系组织评审。

项目设计成绩=商业分析/市场分析成绩（10%）+核心小组座谈纪要成绩（10%）+问卷调查表设计成绩（5%）+SWOT分析成绩（10%）+实施进度表成绩（5%）+实施流程图成绩（5%）+成本核算成绩（5%）+风险分析成绩（10%）+计划书成绩（40%）。（注：此为未取得答辩资格的学生的最终成绩）

最终成绩=项目设计成绩（80%）+答辩成绩（20%）。（此

为参加答辩学生的最终成绩）

从实际出发，建议不硬性要求所有学生参加答辩。但要求考核成绩在良好以上的学生参加答辩，或按比例挑选20%左右的同学参加答辩。此外，论文答辩时要求其他学生必须旁听，至少要让他们了解论文答辩的基本程序。

★建议采用“毕业项目计划设计实施进度表”进行写作全程监管

**英语专业**

**毕业项目计划设计实施进度表**

班级：

| 论文题目 | | | 计划所需总时间（周） | |
|---|---|---|---|---|
| 学生姓名 | | 学号 | 指导老师 | |
| 时间安排 | 写作基本内容 | 项目分解与分值 | 指导老师阶段性评语 | 得分 |
| 第1、2周进行准备工作：Get an overall under-stading of the project. | 指导老师与学生会面，并指导学生学习项目设计实施方案与细则 | 填写论文写作申请表以及开题报告、写作计划等（此项只作参考，无分值） | | |
| 在第3~6周进行选题时完成以下两部分内容：<br>1. What is the problem?<br>2. What is the solution? | 选题阶段：<br>资料收集与商业分析/市场分析 | Analysis of the business (financial situation, current stock movement, real estimates of the finances of the business)（10%） | | |
| | 核心小组会谈纪要 | Focus groups minutes（10%） | | |
| | 问卷调查表设计 | Customer survey design（5%） | | |
| | 强弱机危分析 | SWOT analysis（10%） | | |

| | | | | |
|---|---|---|---|---|
| 第 7~10 周：Plan what you want to do in your project in detail. How will you carry it out? | 项目实施具体计划 | Action plan (5%) | | |
| | 项目实施流程图 | Activity flow chart (5%) | | |
| | 成本核算 | Cost breakdown (5%)<br>a) Premises<br>b) Refurbishment<br>c) Furniture<br>d) Equipment<br>e) Services<br>f) Staff<br>g) Effect on cash-flow | | |
| | 风险分析 | Risk analysis (10%) | | |
| 第 11、12 周：Write the business proposal for your project and hand it in by the end of week 12. | 撰写和提交项目计划书 | Business proposal (40%)<br>a) Content<br>b) Abstract<br>c) Introduction<br>d) Body<br>e) Conclusion<br>f) References<br>g) Appendix | | |
| 注：1. 学生必须在规定的时间内提交八大分项作业和一篇项目计划书。其中缺少任何一项则视为不及格。<br>2. 计划书中每页错误不得超过 10 个，否则视为不及格。 | | | | 总分： |

（说明：此表实为指导老师和学生的任务分解表，无论是学生还是指导老师，都可以参照此表实施各自的任务；指导老师还须在此对学生的每一写作阶段给出阶段性评语和分数，因此，它还是学生成绩评定的重要依据。其他院校使用者可以根据各自不同的专业方向对此表进行灵活处理，切不可生搬硬套。）

★项目设计实施流程建议

一般来说，毕业项目设计启动时间应在毕业前一学期期末布置（即第五学期末），毕业学期（第六学期）完成写作、审核和验收工作。毕业项目设计完成过程（确定选题—安排指导老师—论文审核）不得少于12周。操作流程如下：

第一阶段（2周）：学生独立阅读《商务项目设计指南》，了解商务项目的选题与计划过程，以及每个阶段的要求；在辅导老师的指导下确定项目。

第二阶段（4周）：按照《商务项目设计指南》的要求进行调查分析，完成并上交商业分析、核心小组座谈纪要、问卷调查表设计及SWOT分析四大分项作业；与指导老师商讨所遇到的问题。

第三阶段（4周）：完成并上交项目实施进度表、项目实施流程图、成本核算及风险分析四大分项作业；在辅导老师的指导下，修改并完善所有的分项作业，为撰写项目计划书做好准备。

第四阶段（2周）：完成项目计划书，要求不少于2 500字。

★ 学生必须提交的八大分项作业

学生必须按照项目设计实施流程完成并提交所指定的八大分项作业，指导老师须分别给出初步评价与修改意见并评分（共60分）：

1. 商业分析/市场分析（Analysis of the business）10%
2. 核心小组会谈纪要（Focus groups minutes）10%
3. 问卷调查表设计（Customer survey design）5%
4. SWOT分析（SWOT analysis）10%
5. 项目实施计划表（Action plan）5%
6. 项目实施流程图（Activity flow chart）5%
7. 成本核算（Cost breakdown）5%
8. 风险分析（Risk analysis）10%

特别提示：以上八大分项作业将作为项目计划书中的附录部分，最终必须与计划书一起装订。

以上所提及的无论是写作基本内容、基本原则与要求、考核方式还是实施流程，都具有潜在的变数。而且不同院校的商务英语或应用英语专业所设置的专业建设方向有别，因此建议在确定项目设计的基本内容、原则、要求、考核方式、实施流程时，还需要根据各自不同的专业建设方向作相应的调整。甚至是采用英文还是中文写，是独立完成还是小组共同完成项目设计等，都是值得商榷的。

需要强调的一点是，高职商务英语或应用英语专业的毕业项目设计要以使学生初步了解选择与设计商务项目的全部过程为宗旨，以培养本专业具有相应英语写作水平的合格毕业生为导向，因此考核重在学生参与写作的全过程，而非论文的高质量。

笔者认为，只要我们将毕业项目设计的基本内容、原则与要求以及考核办法等，形成一套较为完整、切实可行的任务驱动型写作系统，在此系统下，使学生严格而规范地按照上述八大具体任务去写作，我们就有理由相信学生的写作将渐渐走上正轨。这样一来，那种盲目抄袭、胡编乱造的现象将会得到有效的遏制；只有这样才能确保学生顺利完成毕业设计任务，同时使他们从中真正学到并巩固专业知识，提高专业英语水平。

# Reference

[1] 杨启宁，崔松. 商务交际英语. 北京：中央广播电视大学出版社，2004.

[2] 胡亦武. 实用商务英语写作. 广州：华南理工大学出版社，2000.

[3] 黄玛莉. 现代商务英文写作. 西安：世界图书出版公司，2004.

[4] John Hilton，羡锡彪. 实用商务项目设计. 北京：中央广播电视大学出版社，2001.

[5] http：//www.ensure.org/guidebook/glossary.htm

[6] http：//www.shop-script.com/glossary.html

[7] http：//www.qualitydigest.com/oct96/surveys.html

[8] http：//www.businessballs.com/swotanalysisfreetemplate.htm

[9] http：//www.geog.leeds.ac.uk/courses/other/casestudies/intra/SWOTanalysis.doc

[10] http：//www.bizhelp24.com/small-business-portal/critical-path-analysis-3.html

[11] http：//www.ider.herts.ac.uk/school/courseware/costs

[12] http：//www.statistics.gov.uk/about/data/guides/LabourMarket/concepts/labour/labourcosts.asp

[13] http：//www.solver.com/risk-analysis

[14] http：//www.4hb.com/0350tipwritebizproposal.html

[15] http：//www.nebs.com/nebsEcat/products/product_ideas/articles/article344/index.jsp

[16] http：//www.scn.org/cmp/modules/pd-smar.htm

# 后 记

我国高等职业学院的崛起，充分体现了国家对职业教育前所未有的重视。而高等职业院校中的商务英语与应用英语专业在众多的专业中独树一帜，以其独特的魅力吸引了众多的学生，为国家培养了一批又一批高素质、高技能的应用型英语人才，为我国的现代化建设作出了突出贡献。

但是，我们也必须清醒地认识到，随着市场经济竞争的日益加剧，人才的争夺也越来越激烈。高职院校赖以生存的特色专业可谓首当其冲。商务英语与应用英语专业在这场严酷的竞争中，步履显得越来越艰辛。因此，如何在逆境中求生存就成了我们这些一线教育工作者的燃眉之急。

教高〔2006〕16号文出台后，高职院校纷纷开始走校企合作之路，课程设置和人才培养模式随之发生了翻天覆地的变化。为了适应这一形势的需要，全国各高职院校纷纷组织商务英语与应用英语专业相关人员深入企业调查研究，了解与掌握企业对本专业人才的需求情况。结果却使大家越发感到，如果还是按以往的英语教育模式培养本专业的学生，无异于作茧自缚，前途黯然。因此痛下决心，摆脱英语教育专业论文写作模式的制约，探寻本专业特色之道成了我们唯一的出路。

作为论文指导老师，笔者可谓饱尝了论文写作模式之苦。其中最主要的原因是学生的写作水平远远达不到这种模式的要求，因此，抄袭成了学生完成论文的主要途径。虽然偶尔有部分学生尝试表现自己的写作水平，但写出来的东西经常文法不通、非驴非马、杂乱无章。有些学生甚至利用翻译软件来应付，结果写出来的论文令指导老师看后莫名其妙，不知所云。另一个原因是论文写作前缺乏应有的指导和计划。其结果是，学生的写作目的不明确，导致学生心猿意马，举棋不定。有些学生到了提交论文的时候，还在其论文的题目上犹豫不决。

可以毫不掩饰地说，这种写作模式根本就无法达到预期的目的和应有的效果。事实表明：这样的写作训练只会培养学生的“抄袭”和“胡诌”技能，而对其专业写作技能的提高毫无益处。因此，对这种所谓毕业论文的写作模式来说，失败是必然的结局，而且毫无意义。

为了扭转这种局面，我们特别组织了一批具有丰富商务英语与应用英语教学经验，并有志于高职院校商务英语与应用英语专业论文写作改革的有志之士编著了这本《商务项目设计指南》，里面包含的章节提供了大量的实例和详细的资料。

本书具有以下几个特点：

(1) 具有很强的针对性。引导学生快捷而准确地选定自己熟悉的或与自己专业相关的项目，这样可以避免学生无的放矢，继而提高写作效率。

(2) 具有很强的操作性。这样易使学生和指导老师把握学习的进度和衡量的尺度。

(3) 具有严密的规划性。使学生在毕业项目设计任务的驱动下，有条不紊地完成阶段性任务。

(4) 具有较大可塑性。可以激发学生的创造意识，拓展学生的想象空间。

(5) 具有较大的可评估性。由于属于项目或任务驱动型的模式，所以更有利于指导老师对学生在各阶段的表现进行评估与考核。

**张海波**

**2015年5月于江门职业技术学院**